THE SLOW JOURNALISM MAGAZINE

ISSUE 34

JAN FEB MAR 2019

Editors
Rob Orchard and Marcus Webb

Art director Christian Tate

Associate editors
Jeremy Lawrence, Matthew Lee
and James Montague

Head of digital Chris Bourn

Head of marketing Vicky Burgess

Subscriptions manager Beverley Milner

Contributors
Matjaz Krivic, Joe Lo, Brian Otieno,
Harriet Salem

Anglo-Finnish liaison officer
Felix Virtanen-Lee

Junior partners
Mila Montague, Freddie and Oscar Orchard,
Barney and Miller Webb

Website design Peter Shepherd, C2 Clear
Creative, c2clearcreative.co.uk

Photographer Jessica Parry

Animator Brendan Cox

Subscription enquiries
subs@slow-journalism.com
or +44 (0)203 865 6082

All other enquiries
hello@slow-journalism.com

The publishers would like to thank
Kate Bouchier-Hayes, Clara Diaz,
Buanassaiva Valentim Lassine,
Scott Lonker, Samussone Manjoge, David
Phillips and all at Makerversity

Cover image
In Its Familiarity, Golden by Grayson Perry

Unless otherwise stated, all images are
supplied by PA or Getty Images

Printed and bound by
Crystal Press, crystalcp.net

**©The Slow Journalism Company,
June 2019**

Delayed Gratification

Slow Journalism matters

Why? Because today's ultra-fast news cycle rates being first above being right. It gives us the beginning of stories but rarely their end. It promotes kneejerk reactions and clickbait journalism over context and perspective. It lends significance to social media nonsense, extreme opinions and celebrity fluff.

We believe in a slower, smarter approach, and with your support we are taking a stand. Each purchase of a copy of **Delayed Gratification** is a vote for non-partisan, independent, intelligent Slow Journalism.

Every issue of the magazine contains investigative reporting, challenging photo features and beautiful infographics which tell the stories others have missed – or mistold. We cut through the white noise and return to the events that matter after the dust has settled.

Armed with three months' worth of hindsight, we aim to capture the times and leave you inspired, informed and thoroughly entertained.

Slow Journalism matters.
We're glad to have you with us.

Rob and Marcus, editors

Delayed Gratification

On the cover: *In Its Familiarity, Golden* by **Grayson Perry**

The work of Turner prize winner, broadcaster and author Grayson Perry is heading to Scotland for the artist's first major solo exhibition in the country. Perry's quartet of tapestries, *Julie Cope's Grand Tour*, will be at the city's Dovecot Studios throughout the summer as part of the 16th Edinburgh Art Festival. Kate Grenyer, Dovecot exhibitions curator, talks to **Matthew Lee** about Grayson's work, the art of tapestry and why everyday lives need to be celebrated.

What can you tell us about *In Its Familiarity, Golden*?

It is a tapestry, part of a series of four which make up *Julie Cope's Grand Tour*. Together they tell the life story of Julie Cope, an Essex everywoman created by Grayson Perry. *In Its Familiarity, Golden* is my favourite of the four. The couple in the middle are Julie and her second husband, Dave. The title's really beautiful because it celebrates the familiarity of a middle-aged marriage, when you know someone and you have that bond. I think there's something really touching about it.

What other elements of the piece are there?

Because it's Grayson Perry, there's a sort of tragedy. It depicts Julie's death in the front right-hand corner. She's been run over by a scooter driven by a man delivering curry. It's a very mundane way to go, but then the everyday is so important to everything that Grayson Perry does.

Why do you think Grayson chose to create the work as a tapestry?

I think one of the reasons Grayson's become so fascinated with tapestries is because they have connotations of being from the castles of kings and they tell stories of chivalry or great battles. They're not necessarily telling tales of an

❶ *In Its Familiarity, Golden* ❷ Grayson Perry

everyday person who has this very ordinary life. But those lives are meaningful. There should be tales about them. The storytelling in this piece is richer than any of his previous tapestries. It's sort of a culmination of his work in tapestry.

The piece will feature as part of Grayson Perry's first major solo show in Scotland. What can we expect for the exhibition?
We wanted to explore both the creative storytelling, but also the technical process that went into this work.

Grayson works with jacquard weaving, a way of making a tapestry using digital technology. We really wanted to expand on the technical craft of it.

What do you think makes him such an important artist?

I think it's the fact that he's such a natural communicator. He is incredibly self aware. He knows that the world of art can get very self-involved and a little bit up itself maybe. He's wonderfully down to earth and people respond to that sincerity.

What other exhibitions at the Edinburgh Art Festival are you looking forward to?

The Edinburgh Printmakers, who have a beautiful new building, are working with someone called Hanna Tuulikki and she's brilliant. I'm look forward to seeing her work. And then Caroline Achaintre at the Edinburgh Sculpture Workshop. She was a rug maker who now creates these woven sculptures. She's very interesting as well. I can't wait. 🔖

Grayson Perry: Julie Cope's Grand Tour: A Crafts Council Touring Exhibition is at Dovecot Studios from 25th July to 2nd November 2019. The Edinburgh Art Festival runs from 25 July to 25 August 2019. For details and tickets see edinburghartfestival.com

In Its Familiarity, Golden, Grayson Perry, 2015. Crafts Council Collection: 2016.19. Acquired with Art Fund support (with a contribution from The Wolfson Foundation) and a donation from Maylis and James Grand. Photo: Stokes Photo Ltd. © Grayson Perry | Portrait: Tristan Fewings/Getty Images

Slow news is good news

Join the Slow Journalism revolution

Buying this magazine is the best way of helping us to swim against the tide of kneejerk news reporting, as every penny we receive is reinvested in quality journalism. But it's not the only way to join the Slow Journalism revolution...

Stay up to date

Fancy some instant *Delayed Gratification*? Head to our blog at slow-journalism.com for in-depth interviews, editorial secrets and our award-winning infographics. You can also sign up for our weekly newsletter, *The Slow Post*

Visit our shop

If you're new to the magazine, you've missed out on some fantastic features over the past eight years. But don't worry: our back issues are available to buy in the DG shop at slow-journalism.com, where you'll also find books, mugs and prints

Attend our events

Learn how to make infographics, become a features writer or launch an independent magazine in our regular classes, or join our journalists for a glass of wine and a chat at our Slow Journalism nights

On the blog

For this issue we sent Harriet Salem to Mozambique to report on how the country is recovering after being hit by two devastating cyclones (see page 108). For video footage of her time there visit the DG blog.

From the archive

It's been a year since the Winter Olympics in Seoul. In issue 30 we got the inside scoop on Korea's unified ice hockey team and asked whether a sporting event could really help end the Korean conflict

Upcoming events

We've just released the tickets for our winter term of classes on infographics, feature writing and launching your own magazine. Tickets are half-price for subscribers. See our website for details.

---

slow-journalism.com/subscribe

Subscribe and **be first** to be 'last to breaking news'

Get the mag before everyone else, with a special subscribers-only cover, delivered to your door anywhere in the world, and help support quality independent journalism

Subscribe and **save 25%** off the single-issue price and **10%** in our shop

That's 480 pages of in-depth, long-form journalism, beautiful photo features and award-winning infographics starting from just £36 per year

Subscribe and **save 50%** off our classes and events

We run regular classes on how to make infographics, how to launch an independent magazine and how to be a features writer. Tickets are half-price for subscribers

Andrew Renneisen/Getty Images | Bruce Bennett/Getty Images | Vicky Burgess

In this issue

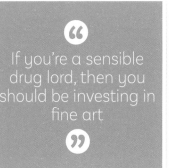

"If you're a sensible drug lord, then you should be investing in fine art"

"It was scary, it was surreal, it was fascinating"

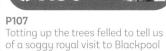

x39

"We had nothing except the clothes we were wearing and our prayers"

JAN

Almanac

The month's news in brief ▼

● EDITED BY: MATTHEW LEE

The story behind the shot

The shoreline of Lake Michigan in Chicago, Illinois, is covered with ice on 30th January as the US midwest experiences one of its worst cold snaps in decades. The polar vortex, which saw temperatures in Chicago fall to a record -29C, was blamed for the deaths of at least 21 people in the US. The extreme cold saw businesses and schools in the Chicago area close, while airlines cancelled nearly 2,600 flights.

Scott Olson/Getty Images

Tue 1st

INDIA ◐ An estimated five million women form a 385-mile human chain across Kerala to campaign for gender equality. The chain was organised by left-wing groups in response to a row over the Sabarimala shrine, which has historically barred access to women aged between 10 and 50. India's supreme court ruled in September 2018 that the shrine's policy was illegal, but women had been unable to enter due to the threat of physical attack. The following day two women aided by police enter the shrine, which prompts violent clashes outside the state parliament.

Wed 2nd

FRANCE ◐ A leader of the *gilets jaunes* is arrested in Paris, signalling a crackdown on the protest movement. Éric Drouet had called for people to gather in Paris in a Facebook video shortly before he was arrested for organising a protest without permission.

US ◐ Netflix urges fans of its film *Bird Box* not to blindfold themselves when performing daily tasks. The warning comes after viewers posted videos of themselves doing the 'Bird Box Challenge', a viral fad inspired by the movie, whose characters cover their eyes to fend off supernatural forces.

Thu 3rd

US ◐ The Democrats take control of the House of Representatives and Nancy Pelosi is elected speaker for the second time in her career.

CHINA ◐ The new Population and Labour Issues report says China's population will start shrinking as soon as 2027.

📖▶ P012
'The great baby bust'

RUSSIA ◐ A former US marine who was arrested in Moscow in December is charged with espionage and may face 20 years in prison if convicted. Russian media report that Paul Whelan was arrested minutes after he was given a USB drive containing classified state information in a Moscow hotel room. Whelan's lawyer later claims that his client believed the USB drive contained only "cultural information".

CHINA ◐ The Chang'e 4 robotic probe becomes the first spacecraft to land on the far side of the moon.

📖▶ P020
'Moment that mattered'

🔔 Bucks to the wall

On 25th January the longest shutdown in US history came to an end after 35 days. It was triggered by Congress's rejection of President Trump's demand for federal funds to build a US-Mexico border wall.

Amount demanded by President Trump to build the border wall

$5.7 billion

$11 billion

Estimated cost of government shutdown to the US economy
Source: Congressional Budget Office

 Fri **4th**

US ◐ The day after assuming office as the youngest US congresswoman in history, Alexandria Ocasio-Cortez – US Representative for New York's 14th congressional district – dances into her office as a response to online trolls

 P022
'The butterfly effect'

Sat **5th**

UK ◐ Consumer group *Which?* **rates Ryanair the worst short-haul airline serving the UK for the sixth year in a row.** The Irish airline calls the survey "worthless".

TURKEY ◐ Ukraine's Orthodox church is granted independence from the Russian church in an Istanbul ceremony. The move by the head of the Eastern Orthodox church, the Ecumenical Patriarch of Constantinople Bartholomew I, provokes fury in Moscow and increases fears of a schism.

Sun **6th**

CUBA ◐ A mysterious noise that caused the American embassy in Havana to withdraw half its staff in 2017 may have only been crickets, according to new research. A scientific analysis of an audio recording of the high-pitched noise, described by US authorities as an 'acoustic weapon' designed to trigger nausea and headaches, revealed that it matched the call of the Indies short-tailed cricket.

US ◐ National security advisor John Bolton says American troops will remain in Syria until Turkey agrees it will not attack Kurdish forces allied to the US. The announcement, made on a visit to Israel, appears to reverse President Trump's stated policy of a withdrawal of all troops by 18th January.

 Mon **7th**

GUATEMALA ◐ The government expels a UN commission investigating alleged government corruption. Foreign minister

---

Record breakers

1,078m
Longest line of sanitary pads
Wed 9th, The all-India convention of gynaecologists, Bengaluru, India

439
Most consecutive bunny hops on a unicycle
Sun 13th, Cole Patterson, Abilene, Texas, US

2,495
Largest gathering of people dressed as scarecrows
Fri 25th, The provincial government of Isabela, Ilagan, Philippines

Sandra Jovel says the panel, which has been investigating president Jimmy Morales and several of his family members over graft allegations, must leave the country.

 Tue **8th**

UK ◐ A 64m-long fatberg is found blocking a sewer in Sidmouth. Made of fat, grease and wet wipes, the congealed mass is taller than the Leaning Tower of Pisa.

 Wed **9th**

NORWAY ◐ Police reveal that the wife of one of the country's richest men has been missing for several weeks. Anne-Elisabeth Falkevik Hagen, the spouse of real estate tycoon Tom Hagen, disappeared on 31st October 2018. Police found a ransom note demanding a payment of €9m to the kidnappers in cryptocurrency. As of June Hagen has still not been found.

Thu **10th**

EGYPT ◐ Mike Pompeo tells a Cairo audience that the US will pursue a more activist policy in the Middle East. The US secretary of state repudiates Barack Obama's legacy in the Middle East, saying the former president had "fundamental misunderstandings" about the region.

Fri **11th**

BELGIUM ◐ A 16th-century painting that is suspected of being a Michelangelo is stolen from a Flemish church. The painting, *The Silence of Our Lady* could be worth up to €100m if its provenance were confirmed.

 P024
'The art of the steal'

Sat **12th**

CANADA ◐ A teenage girl who fled Saudi Arabia and got stranded in Bangkok airport arrives in Toronto. The decision to grant asylum to 18-year-old Rahaf Mohammed al-Qunun, who alleged that her family subjected her to physical and psychological abuse, deepens a diplomatic spat between Canada and Saudi Arabia triggered by Ottawa's criticism of Riyadh's human rights record. Al-Qunun, whose desperate tweets from a Bangkok hotel room alerted the world to her plight, says she has

---

⑪ Crystal balls

What does 2019 have in store for the world? Here's what people across the globe were thinking as the new year began, according to a series of worldwide polls conducted by Ipsos

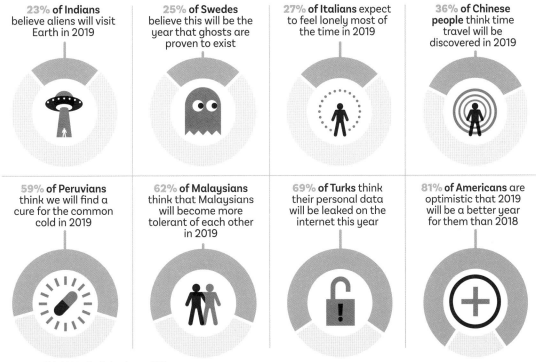

23% of Indians believe aliens will visit Earth in 2019

25% of Swedes believe this will be the year that ghosts are proven to exist

27% of Italians expect to feel lonely most of the time in 2019

36% of Chinese people think time travel will be discovered in 2019

59% of Peruvians think we will find a cure for the common cold in 2019

62% of Malaysians think that Malaysians will become more tolerant of each other in 2019

69% of Turks think their personal data will be leaked on the internet this year

81% of Americans are optimistic that 2019 will be a better year for them than 2018

Source: Ipsos Global Advisor Predictions, January 2019

---

renounced Islam, which is punishable by death in Saudi Arabia.

Sun 13th

POLAND ◎ Gdansk mayor Pawel Adamowicz is stabbed on stage at a charity event. He dies the following day, and a 27-year-old man is charged with his murder. Adamowicz, 53, was known for his criticism of the government's anti-migrant rhetoric.

Mon 14th

IRAN ◎ Nazanin Zaghari-Ratcliffe begins a three-day hunger strike to protest against being refused specialist medical care. The 40-year-old British-Iranian mother, who was jailed in 2016 on spying charges she denies, requires neurological

and psychological care according to her husband, Richard Ratcliffe.

Tue 15th

UK ◎ Theresa May suffers a historic defeat as MPs vote to reject her Brexit deal by a majority of 230. The defeat is the biggest suffered by a government in modern British history.

KENYA ◎ At least 21 people are killed in a terror attack in Nairobi. The 19-hour siege of the DusitD2 compound is claimed by Islamist group al-Shebaab.

Wed 16th

UK ◎ Theresa May's government survives a vote of no-confidence in parliament a day after a huge Brexit defeat.

UK ◎ Leeds United manager Marcelo Bielsa admits that his team has spied on every opposition team this season. The Argentine coach answered questions on the 'Spygate' scandal after Derby County complained that a Leeds staff member was spotted acting suspiciously outside its training ground. Leeds are fined £200,000 by the football league on 18th February.

Thu 17th

UK ◎ Japanese conglomerate Hitachi shelves plans to build a £16 billion nuclear power plant in north Wales due to spiralling costs. The decision, which means that around 9,000 planned jobs will no longer materialise, is viewed as a significant blow to the Welsh economy and the UK

government's plans to develop nuclear energy.

UK ◎ A woman is injured in a car crash caused by Prince Philip near the Sandringham estate in Norfolk. The 97-year-old Duke of Edinburgh, who was unhurt in the collision, later apologises to Emma Fairweather about a lack of communication from the royal family. On 9th February the prince gives up his driving licence.

Fri 18th

GERMANY ◎ A group of leading politicians pens an open letter to the British people, urging the country to stay in the EU. "We would miss the legendary British black humour and going to the pub after work to drink an ale," reads the letter published in *The Times*.

Famous for five minutes

The Gender Balance Index awards,
unbalanced Emirati award ceremony

According to a recent UN report, the UAE ranks highest in the Gulf for gender parity. In 2018, 135,000 Emirati women participated in the labour market, compared with just 1,000 in 1975, and more women held bachelor's degrees than men (43% vs 23%). And who deserves the credit for these great strides towards parity? Middle-aged men, apparently. This year's Gender Balance Index awards didn't feature a single female honoree amongst the winners – a fact not lost on social media where photos of the plaques being dished out to a parade of male officials was roundly mocked. "Wow, really nailed the diversity there," said one user. "One of those dudes was wearing grey". The UAE responded by saying that women had won awards last year.

(Sat) (19th)

DRC ◯ **Félix Tshisekedi's presidential election win is confirmed by the country's constitutional court**, despite opposition leader Martin Fayulu insisting that a secret deal had been made between Tshisekedi and outgoing president Joseph Kabila to deny him victory through electoral fraud. Fayulu's allegations are backed up by a *Financial Times* investigation and analysis of voting data, which showed him winning 59.4 percent compared to Tshisekedi's 19 percent. Tshisekedi denies any wrongdoing.

US ◯ **Students at an all-male private Catholic school in Kentucky come under scrutiny** when footage of them appearing to harass a Native American elder, Nathan Phillips, at an anti-abortion rally in Washington DC goes viral on social media. On 20th January a new video of the incident paints a more complex picture, showing the pupils, who wore pro-Trump hats, being confronted by members of a minor religious movement, the Hebrew Israelites, who appeared to instigate the confrontation with Phillips with their inflammatory rhetoric.

Born

Vegan sausage roll
Hotly-debated snack launched by UK bakery chain Greggs in response to a 2018 petition by PETA signed by more than 20,000 people. Launched **Wed 2nd**

'Dating leave'
A new trend of Chinese companies giving unmarried women over 30 an extra eight holiday days over the Lunar New Year so they can "be in contact with the opposite sex". Reported **Tue 22nd**

'Our Guys in Salisbury'
Russian board game inspired by the Salisbury Novichok attack, created by businessman Mikhail Bober. The aim of the game is to travel from Moscow to Wiltshire without getting stopped by police. Reported **Wed 23rd**

Died

George the snail
The last surviving member of the snail species *Achatinella apexfulva*, 14, **Tue 1st**

Bob Einstein
Comedian best known for playing Marty Funkhouser in *Curb Your Enthusiasm*, 76, **Wed 2nd**

Diana Athill
British editor and novelist, 101 **Wed 23rd**

(Sun) (20th)

SYRIA ◯ **The Israeli military hits Iranian targets near Damascus in an overnight operation in response to rockets fired towards the occupied Golan Heights**. The Syrian army later claims to have shot down the majority of the missiles.

(Mon) (21st)

UK ◯ **Cardiff City footballer Emiliano Sala is killed in a plane crash**. The Argentine striker, who had signed from Nantes two days earlier, was travelling to France to say goodbye to former teammates at the time of the accident. The pilot, David Ibbotson, also dies. Sala's body is later found in the plane's wreckage just off Guernsey.

EARTH ◯ **Stargazers in the Americas and some parts of western Europe are treated to a 'super blood wolf moon'**. The rare lunar eclipse sees the moon glow with a reddish colour and appear bigger and brighter than usual.

(Tue) (22nd)

US ◯ **The Oscars nominations are announced. The Best Picture shortlist draws criticism for including the critically-derided Queen biopic** *Bohemian Rhapsody*.

▦▶ P030
'Oscars vs the people'.

(Wed) (23rd)

GEORGIA ◯ **Police arrest a British fugitive who was convicted of manslaughter**

⏻ Victory   ✖ Defeat

Sun 13th An image of an egg becomes the most-liked Instagram post ever. The plain-looking egg, originally posted by 29-year-old Chris Godfrey, goes on to clock over 53 million likes.

Wed 16th Jasmin Paris becomes the first female winner of the Montane Spine Race, a 268-mile ultra marathon dubbed 'Britain's most brutal race'.

Tue 22nd A Bahamian caterer who was left out of pocket by the organisers of the Fyre Festival raises over $160,000 in a week through crowdfunding. The plight of Maryann Rolle, who used her life savings to pay staff for the event, came to light in a Netflix film about the failed festival.

Mon 7th A Californian man is arrested on suspicion of stealing a winning lottery ticket from his roommate. Police say **Adul Saosongyang** was taken into custody when he attempted to claim the $10m prize.

Tue 15th The EU's Intellectual Property Office strips **McDonald's** of its Big Mac trademark after Irish fast-food chain Supermac's succeeds in a legal battle.

Wed 30th Vegan pop star **Ariana Grande** accidentally has the words 'small charcoal grill' tattooed on the palm of her hand in Japanese. Grande had hoped to have '7 Rings' inked to mark her hit single of the same name, but an error was made in translation.

ⓛ Dark side of the moon vs Pink Floyd

Ⓐ **Thu 3rd** China's Chang'e 4 becomes the first craft to land on the so-called 'dark side of the moon' Ⓑ **Mon 21st** Pink Floyd co-founder Roger Waters lends his private jet to help rescue two young boys from a camp in Syria Ⓒ **Tue 29th** Pink Floyd guitarist David Gilmour says he will auction off more than 120 guitars for charity, including a 1969 Fender used on the album *Dark Side of the Moon*

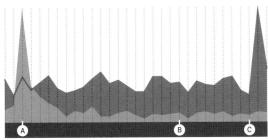

---

when he crashed a speedboat in the River Thames on a first date in December 2015. Jack Shepherd, who went on the run before he was sentenced to six years in prison in July 2018 for the death of Charlotte Brown, handed himself in to a Tbilisi police station. On 10th April Shepherd returns to the UK and is given an extra six months for absconding.

Thu 24th

KENYA ◖ **The UN's Office for Project Services launches a $647 million project to create affordable and sustainable homes in the country.**

📖▶ P032
"This is not a lesser life"

Fri 25th

US ◖ **President Trump agrees to reopen the federal government** after the Senate and House pass a bill to end the longest shutdown in US history.

BRAZIL ◖ **A dam collapses near Brumadinho in Minas Gerais state, releasing nearly 12 million cubic metres of toxic mud and killing at least 237 people**. It is the worst industrial disaster in Brazil's history.

Sat 26th

SPAIN ◖ **The body of a toddler who fell down a well is found after a 13-day rescue effort**. Julen Roselló tumbled into a small unmarked borehole on a private property in Málaga province on 13th January while his parents were making lunch. Rescuers believe the two-year-old didn't survive the 71m drop.

Sun 27th

AUSTRALIA ◖ **Novak Djokovic eases past Rafa Nadal in straight sets to win the Australian Open title**

---

for the seventh time. The previous day's women's final was won by Japanese player Naomi Osaka, whose defeat of Petra Kvitová lifted her to the top of the world rankings.

Mon 28th

BELGIUM ◖ **Nick Clegg announces that Facebook will launch a Dublin "war room" to tackle political misinformation** on the site ahead of European elections in May. In a Brussels speech the firm's head of global policy claims Facebook is entering a "new phase of reform, responsibility and change".

Tue 29th

US ◖ **The justice department files a criminal indictment against Huawei, accusing it of obstructing justice, stealing American technology and committing bank fraud**. The Chinese telecoms company, which is suspected by the US of being used by Beijing for espionage, denies the charges.

Wed 30th

SWITZERLAND ◖ **Footage of a little-known Dutch historian criticising World Economic Forum attendees for avoiding any mention of tax avoidance goes viral on social media**. Speaking on a panel on wealth inequality, Rutger Bregman says that being in Davos feels "like going to a firefighters' conference and not talking about water".

Thu 31st

UK ◖ **The BBC confirms that prime minister Theresa May will not be flying to Brussels in a Spitfire** after the *News at Six* accidentally broadcasts black-and-white World War II footage during a piece on the upcoming Brexit talks. The BBC denies that it was sending out subliminal pro-Brexit messages, blaming "human error" for the mix-up.

The great baby bust

New childbirth figures from China bolster an emerging demographic theory that the world's human population will soon start shrinking, fast. But why has our species taken the collective decision to cull itself? And is there anything we can do to prevent a population crash? ● WORDS: ROB ORCHARD ● ILLUSTRATION: CHRISTIAN TATE

On Thursday 3rd January, four glum-looking representatives of the Chinese Academy of Social Sciences trooped into an anonymous, strip-lit conference room in Beijing to present the 19th annual Population and Labour Issues Report. Despite the minimal fanfare of its launch, it is a surprisingly explosive document.

"For the Chinese population," it states, "the biggest population event in the first half of the 21st century is the arrival of the era of negative population growth." According to the report, if the Chinese continue to reproduce at the same low rate as now, their numbers will plateau in 2027 – three years earlier than previously predicted – and then enter permanent decline. By 2065, China's population will have fallen by 270 million from its peak and there will be far more old people than young.

"Long-term population decline, especially when it is accompanied by a continuously ageing population, is bound to cause very unfavourable social and economic consequences," concludes the report, despondently.

That the most populous nation in history is on course to jettison 18 percent of its citizens in less than 40 years is striking – but these official numbers may even be underestimating the scale of the drop.

The 'replacement' fertility rate at which a society's numbers remain stable is an average of 2.1 births per woman. China's official rate has fallen from 2.75 in 1979 to 1.6 today. "That is half a baby short of what you need to sustain a population," says John Ibbitson, co-author of *Empty Planet: The Shock of Global Population Decline*. "But there are a lot of people who suspect that China's fertility rate may be closer to one, because it is close to one in Japan, South Korea, Taiwan and Singapore. If China's number converges with those of the countries around it, it could lose far more than 300 million people in the course of this century."

Ibbitson, a veteran Canadian journalist, believes that population decline in China will be "one of the dominant narratives of the 21st century."

Family values

New figures published by *The Lancet* in November 2018 show that 91 of the world's 195 countries now have a fertility rate below replacement level, meaning that without substantial immigration their populations are on course to start falling

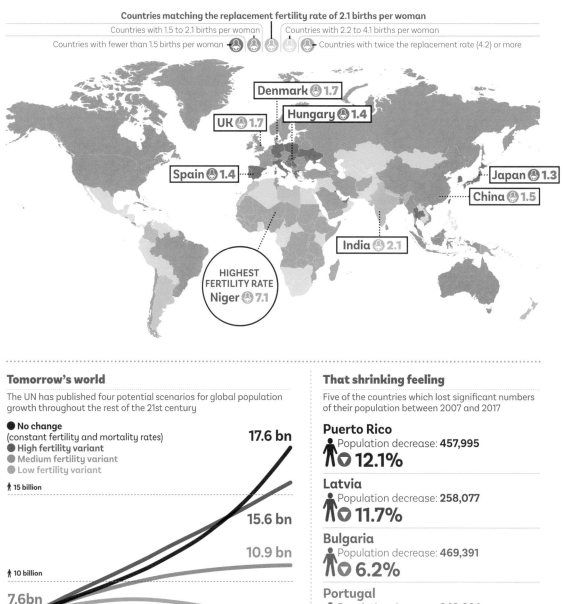

Countries matching the replacement fertility rate of 2.1 births per woman

Countries with 1.5 to 2.1 births per woman | Countries with 2.2 to 4.1 births per woman

Countries with fewer than 1.5 births per woman | Countries with twice the replacement rate (4.2) or more

Denmark 1.7
Hungary 1.4
UK 1.7
Spain 1.4
Japan 1.3
China 1.5
India 2.1

HIGHEST
FERTILITY RATE
Niger 7.1

Tomorrow's world

The UN has published four potential scenarios for global population growth throughout the rest of the 21st century

● **No change**
(constant fertility and mortality rates)
● **High fertility variant**
● **Medium fertility variant**
● **Low fertility variant**

↟ 15 billion

17.6 bn

15.6 bn

10.9 bn

↟ 10 billion

7.6bn

7.3 bn

↟ 5 billion

2020 2030 2040 2050 2060 2070 2080 2090 2100

That shrinking feeling

Five of the countries which lost significant numbers of their population between 2007 and 2017

Puerto Rico
Population decrease: **457,995**
▽ **12.1%**

Latvia
Population decrease: **258,077**
▽ **11.7%**

Bulgaria
Population decrease: **469,391**
▽ **6.2%**

Portugal
Population decrease: **242,664**
▽ **2.3%**

Japan
Population decrease: **1,215,203**
▽ **1%**

"Declining populations are good for some things, but they're really bad for economies," he says. "Starting in about a decade, China will have fewer young people to pay taxes to support older people or to drive consumption by renting apartments or buying cars, all the things that power an economy. If the country does go into a period of prolonged economic stagnation, that could lead to increased unrest. And as we know, there is nothing in the world more dangerous than an empire in decline."

But a precipitous drop in birth rates is not unique to China, whose infamous 'one child' policy, imposed in 1979, was only retired in 2016. The 'Global Burden of Disease' study published in medical journal *The Lancet* in November 2018 showed that fertility rates in 91 of the world's 195 countries now sit below replacement level (it also has China's rate at 1.5). The populations of around two dozen countries are already shrinking. Japan lost almost 450,000 people in 2018 as deaths outstripped births, and the nations of eastern Europe have lost six percent of their collective population since the 1990s, a total of 18 million people.

Despite these falls, the United Nations Population Division's medium variant prediction has the global population continuing to grow to 10.9 billion by 2100, before levelling off. Ibbitson is sceptical of the projections. "It has been at the back of my mind for some time that these UN numbers seemed wonky," he says. "They seemed wonky in 2001 when I wrote my first story about population decline and they seem wonky now." After discovering a body of academic writing questioning the UN narrative on birth figures, he teamed up with Darrell Bricker, CEO of research company Ipsos Public Affairs, and the two travelled the world to try to find the truth about our planet's future occupancy rates.

Their investigation, laid out in meticulous detail in *Empty Planet*, led them to conclude that, far from hitting 10.9 billion, the world's population will peak at nine billion at some point between 2040 and 2060. It will then begin what they describe as "one of the great defining events in human history... a population bust – a relentless, generation-after-generation culling of the human herd."

◐ China's 'one child' policy helped suppress its birth rate, but other countries' rates are also falling

> *China will have fewer young people to support older people or to drive consumption by renting apartments or buying cars*

Empty Spain

In the eastern mountains of Oruense in north-western Spain you can buy an abandoned village with its own cinema, bar and four houses – one of which has 17 bedrooms – for €240,000 (£214,000). Five hours' drive to the east in Burgos you can pick up a deserted village of 75 houses for €425,000 (£379,400). Meanwhile just outside Cuenca, south of Madrid, you can purchase a vacant village with its own church, school, farm, selection of homes, vineyard and warehouse for €1.5 million (£1.38 million). All these offers and dozens more like them are available from Aldeas Abandonadas (Abandoned Villages), one of a host of estate agencies selling unoccupied villages across depopulated rural areas of the country.

The largest of these areas is referred to as España Vacía – Empty Spain. "We are talking about the most extensive continuous territory affected by depopulation in the Iberian peninsula," says Dr Carme Melo, a lecturer in the geography department of the University of Valencia. "Empty Spain includes five different autonomous regions with around 1,200 towns and covers 63,000 square kilometres. Parts of it are referred to in the media as the 'Spanish Lapland' because they are so sparsely populated."

Spain's answer to Santa's homeland has been created by the migration of millions of people over multiple generations from the countryside to the city. "People left because of a lack of decent housing, basic services and employment opportunities – particularly for women," says Melo. "It started with the enclosure and privatisation of land in the 18th century, then industrialisation, the growth of the cities and the mechanisation of agriculture. And then there is the idea, reinforced throughout the centuries, that the city is synonymous with culture, opportunity and development, and that the countryside just holds us back. In the social imagination the idea that the countryside is less important than the city is very powerful. All these forces have led to the depopulation of this huge area."

While Empty Spain is at the extreme end of depopulation, the phenomenon of urbanisation that created its bargainous deserted villages has been repeated across the world. Researchers at the North Carolina State University and the University of Georgia calculated that on 23rd May 2007, for the first time ever, there were more humans living in urban than rural environments. And when humans move to the cities one of the first things they do, after complaining about the size of the apartments and learning not to talk to people on public transport, is to stop having so many children.

"In a rural environment, children are economic assets," says Ibbitson. "You can put them to work in the fields. In the city, they're just an economic drain, another mouth to feed. In cities women have access to education, which leads to empowerment, which leads them to conclude that they don't want to have as many children as their mother had." Religion – particularly of the go-forth-and-multiply variety – also factors in. "Organised religion is more powerful in rural environments than it is in urban environments," says Ibbitson. "Then there's the declining power of the clan. In the village, you're surrounded by your extended family, all those aunties urging you to get married and have children. In the urban environment, you're surrounded by office workers. When was the last time one of your co-workers urged you to have a baby?"

"These things combine, with the result that if you and your partner decide to have a child, you're not having it for economic advantage or because God or your family tell you you must. You're having it because you and your partner want to. It is an act of personal fulfilment – but as it turns out, people are very quickly fulfilled. One or two kids is usually enough." Spain's own fertility rate currently stands at 1.4. Its population began shrinking in 2011, and its institute of national statistics predicts that on current trends it will lose half a million people in the next 15 years and 5.4 million by 2066.

Ibbitson and Bricker believe the UN is underestimating the effects of urbanisation on birth rates. "Urbanisation is accelerating and as a result of that acceleration birth rates that took a century and a half to decline in the developed world are plummeting in a single generation in the developing world," says Ibbitson. "The UN has India at 2.3, but demographers we talked to in the country suspect that it's actually closer to 2.1, that the data's out of date. The new *Lancet* study has India at 2.1 – replacement rate. I think that's the sort of thing we should stand up and wave our arms around about. The world's second largest country is not going to be a generator of a whole lot of babies going forward."

> ❝
> Having a child is an act of personal fulfilment – but as it turns out, people are very quickly fulfilled
> ❞

Baby drivers

In 2013, Eva Lundgren saw an article in a Danish newspaper that caught her attention. "It wasn't front page stuff," she says. "It was more like page ten, a story about Denmark's birth rate and how it could make problems in our welfare system, which we Danes are very proud of. It said that with the birth rate declining we wouldn't be able to have the support for the elderly in the future that we have today."

Lundren works as head of marketing for Spies, a Danish travel company owned by Thomas Cook Northern Europe, and decided she could help boost Denmark's 1.7 birth rate at the same time as getting her brand some useful exposure. And so 'Do it for Denmark' was born. The campaign consisted of a series of adverts setting out Denmark's demographic problem and suggesting that Danes might like to fix it by going on holiday and having sex with their partner. It increased Spies' sales by 40 percent.

In addition, women could go onto the Spies site, put in the date of their period, and automatically be sent special promotional deals for city getaways on days when they would be ovulating. Should their mini-break result in a pregnancy, they could send a doctor's report of the due date to Spies to be entered into a competition to win three years' worth of baby supplies and a kid-friendly holiday. "We thought nobody would enter," says Lundgren, "I mean, the requirements were pretty high. You had to be pregnant to take part. But seven people did."

Do it for Denmark also helped to get the issue of falling birth rates onto the national agenda. "I think we pushed the ball, and it started rolling, and then somebody else pushed it as well, and we all got a higher awareness to the problem and how serious it was if we didn't do something about it," says Lundgren. The city of Copenhagen produced a pro-conception campaign and a documentary entitled "Knald for Danmark" ("Screw for Denmark") was broadcast on national TV.

Then in 2015, after dropping constantly over many years, the birth rate registered a little uptick. "That was very joyful for us," says Lundgren. Her follow-up campaign, entitled Do it for Mom, focused on how sad Danish mothers of grown-up children would be if they did not become grandmothers. The proposed solution, unsurprisingly, was to encourage their offspring to go on holiday and have sex with their partner.

YouTube

10%

UNDFANGET PÅ FERIE

10% of all Danish children are conceived on holidays.

So to help the falling Danish birthrate,

Spies Travel wants to encourage all Danes

to take a romantic city holiday.

○ ○ Stills from the 'Do it for Denmark' campaign video by the Spies travel agency, which focused on the country's falling birthrate and suggested a city break-based solution

Book your holiday with our ovulation discount.

And prove you conceived a child

to win a 3-year supply of baby stuff.

DO IT FOR DENMARK

It's not just Danish travel agencies that are trying to fix the imminent collapse of the human population, however. In February 2019 Viktor Orbán, the prime minister of Hungary (birth rate 1.4), announced that women who have four or more children will be exempt from income tax for the rest of their lives. In Italy (birth rate 1.3) the government is introducing a programme to give free farmland to women who have a third child. Meanwhile, Spain has created the official position of Commissioner of the Government against the Demographic Challenge (predictably dubbed a 'Sex Tsar' by British tabloids) to co-ordinate attempts to increase its birth rate.

Ibbitson believes that none of these gambits – or more standard actions like increasing paternity leave or offering free childcare – are likely to have a significant effect. "They're not successful because of something called the low fertility trap," he says. "Simply put, once your society has a low birthrate, it gets used to having one." Ibbitson believes that immigration is the only way for countries with insufficient babymakers to keep their population topped up. "We realise that it is very difficult for some countries to simply accept large numbers of immigrants, but you must accept them if you want to continue to grow your economy," he says.

This will not sit well with Orbán, who commented while he was introducing his eternal tax-break for fecund Hungarians that "Migration for us is surrender." "Perpetual decline is also surrender, is it not?", says Ibbitson.

Immigration will not solve the broader problem of global population decline, and may even make it worse in the long term. When people emigrate from a place with a high fertility rate to one with a low fertility rate, they tend to adapt their baby expectations within a generation of their arrival. "If you leave the Philippines [birth rate 3.1] and come to Canada, you're leaving one world view and arriving in a completely different one," says Ibbitson. "Even if you decide to retain some of the world view of the place you left, your children certainly won't. They will grow up in Canada and they will have modern Canadian values, and they will have the 1.6 children that Canadians have on average."

◐ Viktor Orbán, prime minister of Hungary, announces his new babymaking plan

“

Hungarian women who have four or more children will be exempt from income tax for the rest of their lives

”

Fewer, older, greener, kinder

A world with increasingly few young people would not be all bad. While there would be economic challenges, there would be fewer problems with youth unemployment, as young people became a precious resource (although they might have to pay almost all of their wages over in tax to support an ever-greater percentage of old-timers). Instead of trying to deter young immigrants from arriving in their countries, governments might start to actively court them in order to maintain productivity levels.

Should climate change not become irreversible before the global population tops out, then greenhouse gas emissions ought to start shrinking every year afterwards. The positive effect on the environment will be further enhanced by ever-increasing urbanisation which will allow marginal farmland to be rewilded. "In every way, shape and form, a declining human population is great for the planet itself and something to celebrate," says Ibbitson, although he's keen to emphasise that his research should not be used "as a manual for climate change scepticism." "We are talking about decades out," he says.

An ageing world may even bring with it what Ibbitson describes as a "geriatric peace", with fewer testosterone-fuelled young men to join extremist groups, sign up for patriotic wars or headbutt one another in suburban pub car parks. But it may also be less innovative. "Young people tend to come up with all the good ideas," says Ibbitson. "On the other hand, we're still going to have large young populations in Africa and India for decades to come, so we may find that the innovation and creativity starts to centre around places like Lagos and Mumbai."

If Ibbitson and Bricker's theory is right, though, alongside economic and social upheaval, within most of our lifetimes we'll also have to deal with a radical shift in our self-image as a species. "The coming change has never happened before in the history of humanity," says Ibbitson. "There have been calamities, wars and famines that have reduced our numbers, but we've never deliberately decided, through individual decisions, collectively to do so. I wonder how it will feel to be a race that's chosen to get older and get smaller – possibly forever." ◉

LEARN

The Delayed Gratification team teach regular classes in **infographics, features writing** and **how to launch an independent magazine.**

For our schedule of upcoming classes and events visit **slow-journalism.com/events-and-classes**

Thu 3rd **JAN** 2019

Moment that mattered

China's space agency lands a probe on the far side of the moon

Andrew Coates, professor of physics,
Department of Space, UCL ● INTERVIEW: ROB ORCHARD

The Chinese national space agency (CNSA) successfully landed its Chang'e 4 lunar module on the far side of the moon on 3rd January. It was the first mission of its kind – all previous lunar landings have taken place on the near side.

Andrew Coates, a UCL physics professor who works on the European Space Agency's ExoMars rover, was impressed. "Chang'e 4 brought China to the top table of real international space power," he says. "It's a powerful demonstration to be able to land anywhere on the far side of the moon, with all the difficulties of communication involved." Direct transmissions from the far side are impossible – the moon is in the way – so in May 2018 the Chinese team launched a special communication satellite, Queqiao, which relayed signals from Earth to the module from its position 65,000 kilometres beyond the moon.

Chang'e 4's mission is to discover more about the far side of the moon. "They're trying to understand the South Pole-Aitken basin, which is a big impact crater, and do some geophysical and solar wind interaction measurements," says Coates. The 1,600-mile diameter, eight mile-deep South Pole-Aitken basin was chosen for touchdown because it's thought to contain material from the moon's interior mantle, thrown up by whatever gigantic space projectile once smashed into it with such force. To analyse samples of this mantle Chang'e 4 released a rover, Yutu 2, which has already started sending back data – although as it is solar-powered and the lunar night lasts for 14 days, it does have regular fortnight-long breaks in transmission while it goes into low power mode.

As well as Yutu 2, Chang'e 4 carried a temperature-regulated 'mini lunar biosphere' canister containing seeds from Earth and on 15th January, the *People's Daily*, part of the Chinese state media, shared a photo of a cotton plant sprouting aboard the module in what it claimed was "humankind's first biological experiment on the moon." Sadly the cotton couldn't stay the course. A day after the big announcement, state media broke the news that the first Earth plant to germinate on the moon had died.

"That was a very small-scale experiment just to examine whether it's possible to grow plants on the moon," says Coates. "Potentially it might be useful in developing moon bases, which various space agencies are now talking about. The US and Europe are working on the Deep Space Gateway, a proposed space station in orbit around the moon, which would enable some lunar science and potentially a human outpost which might eventually spread to the surface." Surface bases could be used for extraterrestrial mining, or even for the creation of solar power stations on the moon, where panels could produce up to 40 times more electricity than their earthbound equivalents. In an early proof of concept, the Chinese government reportedly plans to launch a solar power station into orbit around the Earth by 2025.

The CNSA made use of instruments specially created for its mission by an international coalition of scientists and engineers from the Netherlands, Germany, Sweden and Saudi Arabia. "One of the really nice things about space science is that we can transcend the political boundaries, and do collaboration in space to everybody's benefit," says Coates.

> **"One of the really nice things about space science is that we can transcend the political boundaries"**

The exorbitant cost of space exploration means that it makes sense for countries to team up and to develop complementary niches. Even countries whose politicians are at loggerheads find ways to cooperate in the final frontier. While China and the US were ramping up a tit-for-tat trade war and President Trump was accusing Chinese tech company Huawei of commercial espionage in late 2018, Nasa was working with information from CNSA to guide its Lunar Reconnaissance Orbiter to observe the Chang'e 4's touchdown and analyse the "signature" of the plume of dust thrown up by its landing.

For all that the Chang'e 4 has brought prestige and new scientific opportunities to the Chinese, it is, says Coates, just the start. "It's really a sort of technology demonstration," he says. "It's part of a phased programme to do moon landings, and then go off and land somewhere else." The next step is Mars – and the Chinese won't be alone. "In the planned flotilla of spacecraft going to Mars in 2020, as well as the Chinese orbiter and rover, there will be one from the UAE, the American Mars 2020 rover and the European Space Agency's ExoMars Rover," says Coates.

In June, India announced that it would be attempting a soft landing of a moon rover in September, which would make it only the fourth country ever – behind the US, Russia and now China – to touch down on the lunar surface. Until then, the Yutu 2 will be alone, trundling its way across the lunar surface, a potent symbol of a nation with serious future ambitions in space. ⓐ

AFP/Getty Images

The butterfly effect

How the 1830 flight of a Russian grand duke in drag led to America's youngest congresswoman dancing in the halls of the Capitol in 2019

● WORDS: ROB ORCHARD ● ILLUSTRATION: CHRISTIAN TATE

Sources: BBC, Billboard, BU Today, 'Cholera: A Worldwide History' by SL Kotar and JE Gessler, 'The Death of Franz Liszt' by Alan Walker, Encyclopaedia Britannica, habsburger.net, Hyperion Records, *The New Yorker*, RFI, UCLA Fielding School of Public Health

🦋 29th November 1830

Grand Duke Constantine, the Russian viceroy of Poland and brother of Tsar Nicholas I, is forced to flee Warsaw disguised in women's clothing after a group of Polish army cadets storms his residence with the aim of assassinating him. The event marks the beginning of the 'November Uprising' against Russian control.

🦋 25th January 1831

The Polish parliament passes an act of dethronisation, deposing Nicholas I as king of Poland. Furious at this defiance and the humiliation of his brother, Nicholas sends his army to invade. On 4th February, 115,000 Russian soldiers cross into Poland. There has been an outbreak of Asiatic cholera in Russia which the soldiers bring with them.

🦋 February 1831

Cholera takes hold in Poland and swiftly spreads westwards across Europe, arriving in Hungary in June, Germany in August and Britain in October. Seeing the disease advance towards their populations, panicked authorities in cities along the way erect barriers and restrict movement, while citizens sprinkle their houses with holy water.

🦋 March 1832

The pandemic reaches Paris and within two weeks an estimated 7,000 people have died from cholera, which continues to ravage the city for six months.

🦋 22nd April 1832

Virtuoso Italian violinist Niccolò Paganini performs a benefit concert for people affected by cholera in Paris. In the audience is 20-year-old Hungarian piano teacher Franz Liszt who is mesmerised by Paganini's dramatic performance and resolves to become the 'Paganini of the piano'. He begins practising intensely, honing a flamboyant style and new techniques.

🦋 27th December 1841

Liszt gives a recital at the Sing-Akademie in Berlin, where he is greeted rapturously by the crowd. His reception at subsequent concerts becomes increasingly hysterical: audience members faint, sob, scream and fight over his discarded handkerchiefs. Poet and essayist Heinrich Heine coins the term 'Lisztomania' to describe this reaction to the handsome pianist.

🦋 7th July 2009

French indie pop band Phoenix releases the single 'Lisztomania', inspired by the pianist's extraordinary popularity. The video for the song features the band members having fun at the Franz Liszt Museum and other Liszt-themed locations in Bayreuth.

🦋 September 2011

A group of Boston University students, including international relations and economics undergraduate Alexandria Ocasio-Cortez, shoot a video of themselves dancing on the roof of the Arts and Sciences building to the sound of 'Lisztomania'. They post it on YouTube.

AnonymousQ1776
@AnonymousQ1776

Here is America's favorite commie know-it-all acting like the clueless nitwit she is...
...High School video of "Sandy" Ocasio-Cortez @AoDespair

1:10 PM - 3 Jan 2019

🦋 3rd January 2019

Democrat Alexandria Ocasio-Cortez, now known as AOC, is sworn in as the youngest congresswoman in US history. On the same day an anonymous poster on Twitter shares a 30-second edit of the Boston University rooftop dance accompanied by the phrase "Here is America's favorite commie know-it-all acting like the clueless nitwit she is."

🦋 July 1886

Liszt is taken ill while visiting his daughter Cosima in Bayreuth, Germany. Lina Schmalhausen, a besotted pupil and companion to the 74-year-old, is banished from the house by Cosima and sleeps under a bush in the garden. After Liszt dies on the 31st, Cosima allows Lina to place a posy of forget-me-nots in his hand. He is buried in the municipal cemetery and a museum is later set up in his honour in the town.

🦋 4th January 2019

The video goes viral and is viewed almost two million times in less than 48 hours. It fails to elicit the hoped-for condemnation of AOC, with the vast majority of posters finding it charming. In response, AOC tweets a video of herself dancing into her new Capitol Hill office alongside the words "Wait till they find out Congresswomen dance too!"

The art of the steal

From the theft of the *Mona Lisa* in 1911 to the "lost Michelangelo" stolen from a Belgian church in January 2019, art crimes have often captured the public's imagination. But while such heists may conjure up images of the *Thomas Crown Affair*, the reality of looted masterpieces is far less romantic ● WORDS: MARCUS WEBB

"There was an alarm in the church, but it was very old and kept going off and annoying the neighbours," says Jan Van Raemdonck ruefully. "So we turned it off. We have a separate museum with a working alarm – maybe I should have put the painting in there?"

Van Raemdonck is a priest in the small Flemish town of Zele, 45 miles north of Brussels. When he first took up the position in 2018, he discovered a painting hidden away behind the high altar of his new church. Older than most of the pictures in the Baroque building and painted on board, the image of the baby Jesus asleep on Mary's knee fascinated Van Raemdonck. An amateur historian, he began to look into the story behind *The Silence of Our Lady*.

Van Raemdonck's investigations led him to the collection of the Duke of Portland in the UK, where he discovered a 1538 Michelangelo sketch which he believed to be "remarkably similar" to *The Silence of Our Lady*. If Michelangelo had used that sketch as the basis for the painting, then the church would be in possession of a masterpiece worth millions. It's a big if. "There are only five known Michelangelo paintings on board," concedes Van Raemdonck. "The idea that there was a sixth one here in Belgium seemed impossible. But I believed it was by him or one of his students." Despite his excitement, Van Raemdonck shared his discovery with only a handful of people, including respected Michelangelo expert Maria Forcellino. Days before Forcellino was due to appraise the piece the church, with its annoying and consequently deactivated alarm, was broken into and the painting stolen.

The Mystery of Zele is the latest in a long line of art heists stretching back through history. On 21st August 1911 Vincenzo Perruggia, an Italian decorator, emerged from the cupboard where he had been hiding all night, prised the *Mona Lisa* from her frame and walked out of the Louvre with her hidden under his coat. The blitz of publicity around the theft turned the portrait into a sensation. Queues formed outside the museum for the

◗ Jan Van Raemdonck in front of *The Silence of Our Lady* before the 'lost Michelangelo' was stolen
◗ Police tape surrounds Strängnäs Cathedral, Sweden, following the theft of royal jewels, July 2018

first time as people lined up just to see the empty space where the painting had once hung. By the time it was recovered two years later, the *Mona Lisa* was the most famous painting in the world.

While *The Silence of Our Lady* is unlikely to reach similar levels of fame, its theft did attract international headlines, with the *Guardian* declaring it a case "worthy of a Hercule Poirot whodunnit". Speculation circled about a sophisticated art thief stealing works to order, but Van Raemdonck has a more prosaic explanation. "I suppose it was somebody from the town," he says with a sigh. "They probably stole it, sold it and spent the money on drugs." Speculation has now died down and the investigation has gone quiet: Van Raemdonck says he hasn't heard from the police working on the case in a month. "Let's hope that whoever took it will repent their deeds and bring it back," he says.

A bin full of crown jewels

While sceptical that *The Silence of Our Lady* is a lost Michelangelo, art expert Will Korner believes that it is perfectly possible it may reappear on the church's doorstep. "Criminals often realise that publicity has made a stolen object too hot to handle," he says citing the theft of the Swedish crown jewels in July 2018 from Strängnäs Cathedral. "The press loved that story – it involved a speedboat chase and some literal daylight robbery," says Korner. "But when the jewels were recovered in February 2019 it didn't make the same splash."

The criminals returned the jewels in a novel fashion, placing them in a dustbin, with the word 'bomb!' painted on the side. They placed the bin on top of a car before calling the authorities, who thankfully chose not to carry out a controlled explosion and blow Charles IX's stolen funeral regalia to kingdom come. "The thieves clearly came to the conclusion that they couldn't really do anything with the jewels," says Korner. "If it had been me, I would have broken them down - sold off a few diamonds at a time, melted down the precious metals... That's what they should have done. You learn a lot when you're on this side of the desk."

Korner's "side of the desk" is helping to run the Art Loss Register (ALR) the world's largest private database of lost and stolen art, antiques and collectables. Set up by art and insurance professionals in 1990, the database now covers over half a million registered items. This vast index works as the art world's due diligence service – for a fee

> **"** I would have broken the crown jewels down – sold a few diamonds at a time, melted the precious metals... **"**

ALR will allow buyers and sellers to check any suspicions of illegitimate ownership before a work is sold, in order to avoid legal complications. It has a pretty good track record: since launch it has helped with the recovery of stolen items worth over £500 million.

These are usually lower-profile pieces than potential Michelangelos. "We tend to deal with the cases that don't make the papers," says Korner. "The objects aren't that interesting to the media as they're not that valuable – normally around the £10,000 mark - but they mean a hell of a lot to the people who originally owned them." According to Korner, at any one time the team is checking on the legal status of 150 artworks. "Hopefully as our net gets bigger, as it has done every year, we're not only disincentivising the actual theft, but lowering the value of what you would get if you stole an object."

As well as the best way to strip a Swedish crown for parts, Korner's time at ALR has taught him that the reality of art crimes is a long way from the evocative headlines they can generate. "This isn't *The Thomas Crown Affair* with suave thieves pinching masterpieces in ingenious ways," he says. "Most art crimes are opportunistic. The works are usually stolen by petty thieves during break-ins and then sold or passed along the criminal chain to larger criminal organisations that deal in drugs, human trafficking, weapons... It's not this glamorous Hollywood-ised venture that a lot of people make it out to be."

According to Korner, the vast majority of stolen artworks will be sold at flea markets or small auction houses for a fraction of what they are worth. If a painting is discovered to be particularly valuable then it is usually returned or ends up in the hands of organised criminal gangs who may put it aside for use as a future bargaining chip. "There have been cases in Italy where mafiosi have been arrested and, in return for a reduced sentence, they have led law enforcement to stolen objects," says Korner. "Whenever an old masterpiece that's been missing for decades miraculously turns up under some grandmother's bed or in an attic I'm suspicious that it's the result of a deal like this."

A painting doesn't even need to be stolen in order to help fund organised crime. "Artworks can sell for millions of dollars," says Korner. "If you're a sensible drug lord, then you should be investing in fine art. Buying a painting in one country and moving it to another to sell is a fantastic way of cleaning dirty cash. For some reason, when it comes to art, people do not ask the same questions that banks and property lawyers do. Let's say you buy a Picasso for

$10 million, and then you sell it for $8 million, I think most people involved in organised crime would be very happy to take that for laundered cash."

Looting on an industrial scale

The majority of working hours at the Art Loss Register today are still spent dealing with pieces stolen during the Third Reich over 70 years ago. We may have to wait a similar time to understand the consequences of modern day perpetrators of industrial-scale looting.

"I think it will be years, maybe decades, before we discover the scale of theft from Iraq and Syria under Isis," says Leila Amineddoleh. An art and cultural heritage lawyer, Amineddoleh says the majority of items coming out of Isis-controlled territories in recent years are antiquities, which can be even harder to identify than looted art. "You can usually trace an artwork back to a prior owner," she says. "Picasso did this work, it went to his dealer, it was sold to this person and so on. Looted antiquities are different. They're from the ground. We often don't know where they came from, even the country. People talk about Roman objects, that might not mean modern-day Italy. Roman objects are found as far north as Scotland. The sad reality is that the majority of looted objects will not be returned to their home country."

While Isis's highly publicised attempted destruction of ancient sites such as Palmyra made for some useful propaganda for the 'caliphate', Amineddoleh believes that archaeological objects of value were more likely to be sold to fund the cause than to be destroyed. "We've found tunnels full of antiquities in former Isis territories," she says. "If they were destroying antiques because

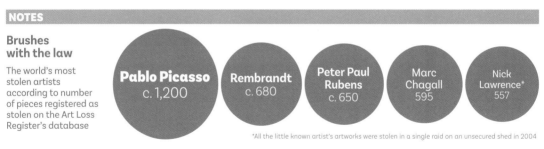

○ A Babylonian boundary stone, looted from Iraq and seized at Heathrow airport in 2012, is handed back to Iraq in March 2019

> **"**
> I think it will be years, maybe decades, before we discover the scale of theft from Iraq and Syria under Isis
> **"**

they thought they were idolatrous, then why wouldn't everything be destroyed? The thought is that they were hoping to get them on to the western market, because that's where the value is." This value only exists because somebody is buying – usually a dealer who's willing to play the long game.

"At the moment everyone's on high alert, people are naturally suspicious of objects coming out of Syria or Iraq," says Amineddoleh. "Still, there are individuals spending hundreds of thousands, if not millions of dollars, on these rare pieces. They will put them in warehouses and wait until there is the opportunity to sell them later down the line, when Isis has become just a memory."

Some collectors argue that by buying these looted objects, dealers and art lovers are saving pieces – getting them out of the hands of would-be destroyers and preserving them for future generations. Amineddoleh has little time for such rationales. "I believe purchasing loot incentivises looting," she says. "If you're buying these stolen antiquities, then looters know that there's a market. These pieces are not being extracted by a trained archaeologist, they are being ripped out of the ground. They are destroying these archaeological sites, destroying the heritage, destroying history. I wish more people would recognise that and think past, 'I want this object. I love it. I want it in my collection'."

Back in Zele, pastor Jan Van Raemdonck is working on a book about the missing painting he loves. With no insurance, he lives in hope that the work will be returned. "It is an object of devotion," he says. "People came to pray before it. People felt close to the holy family when they were close to that painting. It deserves better than this." ⊕

How to cash in on celebrity diets

On Quitters' Day, the day on which people are most likely to give up New Year's resolution diets, Evil Stick Man becomes a fat cat from slimming

● WORDS: MARCUS WEBB ● ILLUSTRATION: CHRISTIAN TATE

1

Approach a relatable C-list celebrity. Have them sign a contract agreeing to follow your specific instructions on their lifestyle over six months.

2

For the first three months have your celebrity consume twice the daily recommended calorie intake and avoid sunlight, vitamins and soap.

3

At the end of this period arrange for your celebrity to take a holiday in an unglamorous location and have an unskilled photographer take poorly-lit, unflattering shots of them at the beach.

4

For the next three months have your celebrity consume half the daily recommended calorie intake and pay for them to have personal training and sunbed sessions.

5

Send your now-svelte celebrity on holiday in a glamorous location – paid for by a publicity-hungry tourist board – and get beautifully-lit shots of them frolicking on the beach in full makeup.

6

Sell the original, unflattering shots to a celebrity magazine and provide quotes from a 'friend' about how the celebrity has turned to eating to mend their broken heart.

7

Two weeks later, sell the flattering shots to the same magazine with a story about how a miraculous diet and exercise routine has helped resurrect the celebrity's body and mind.

8

Release a series of fitness/cookery/mindfulness books and DVDs by your celebrity, propelling them to A-list status and your books and DVDs up the charts.

9

You are now rich. Hire Jane Fonda and Mr Motivator as your live-in personal trainers

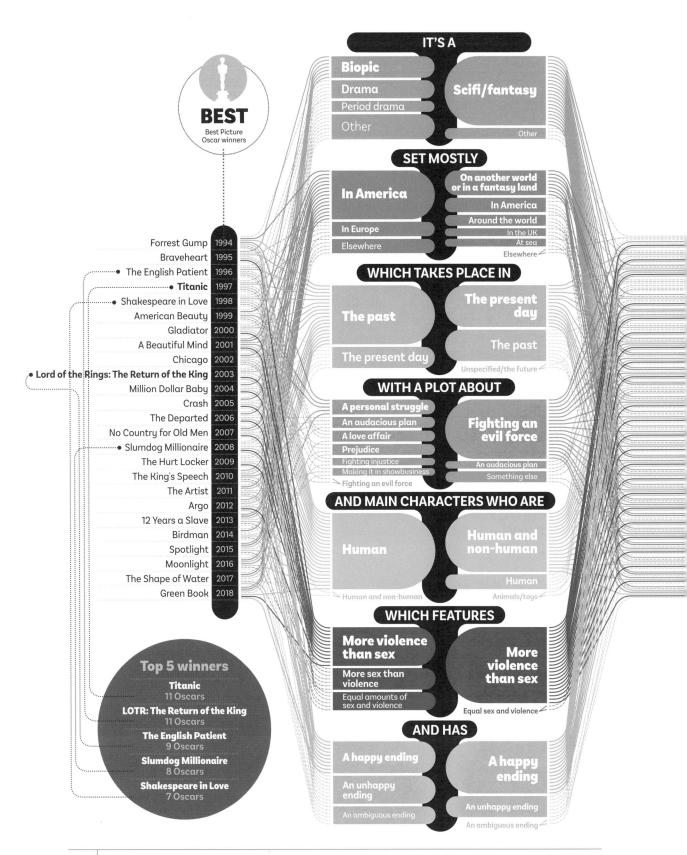

BEST

Best Picture
Oscar winners

Forrest Gump	1994
Braveheart	1995
The English Patient	1996
Titanic	1997
Shakespeare in Love	1998
American Beauty	1999
Gladiator	2000
A Beautiful Mind	2001
Chicago	2002
Lord of the Rings: The Return of the King	2003
Million Dollar Baby	2004
Crash	2005
The Departed	2006
No Country for Old Men	2007
Slumdog Millionaire	2008
The Hurt Locker	2009
The King's Speech	2010
The Artist	2011
Argo	2012
12 Years a Slave	2013
Birdman	2014
Spotlight	2015
Moonlight	2016
The Shape of Water	2017
Green Book	2018

Top 5 winners

Titanic
11 Oscars

LOTR: The Return of the King
11 Oscars

The English Patient
9 Oscars

Slumdog Millionaire
8 Oscars

Shakespeare in Love
7 Oscars

IT'S A

Biopic
Drama
Period drama
Other
Scifi/fantasy
Other

SET MOSTLY

In America
On another world or in a fantasy land
In America
Around the world
In the UK
At sea
In Europe
Elsewhere
Elsewhere

WHICH TAKES PLACE IN

The past
The present day
The past
The present day
Unspecified/the future

WITH A PLOT ABOUT

A personal struggle
An audacious plan
A love affair
Prejudice
Fighting injustice
Making it in showbusiness
Fighting an evil force
Fighting an evil force
An audacious plan
Something else

AND MAIN CHARACTERS WHO ARE

Human
Human and non-human
Human
Human and non-human
Animals/toys

WHICH FEATURES

More violence than sex
More sex than violence
Equal amounts of sex and violence
More violence than sex
Equal sex and violence

AND HAS

A happy ending
An unhappy ending
An ambiguous ending
A happy ending
An unhappy ending
An ambiguous ending

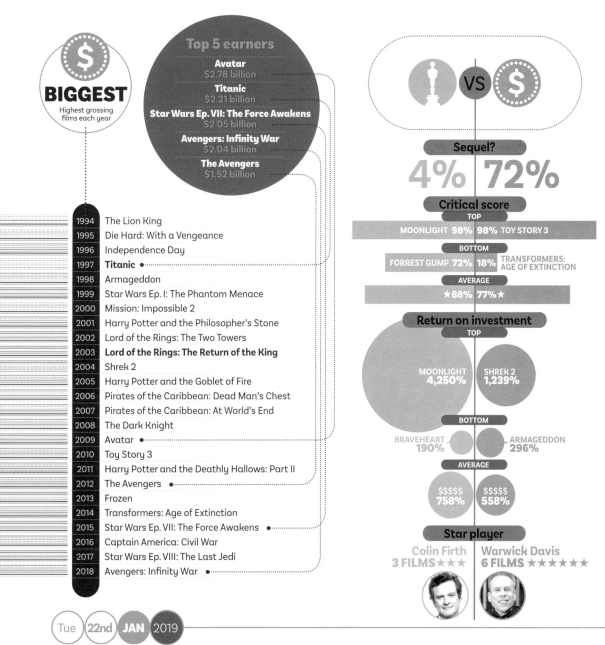

BIGGEST
Highest grossing films each year

Top 5 earners

Avatar
$2.78 billion

Titanic
$2.21 billion

Star Wars Ep. VII: The Force Awakens
$2.05 billion

Avengers: Infinity War
$2.04 billion

The Avengers
$1.52 billion

1994	The Lion King
1995	Die Hard: With a Vengeance
1996	Independence Day
1997	**Titanic** •
1998	Armageddon
1999	Star Wars Ep. I: The Phantom Menace
2000	Mission: Impossible 2
2001	Harry Potter and the Philosopher's Stone
2002	Lord of the Rings: The Two Towers
2003	**Lord of the Rings: The Return of the King**
2004	Shrek 2
2005	Harry Potter and the Goblet of Fire
2006	Pirates of the Caribbean: Dead Man's Chest
2007	Pirates of the Caribbean: At World's End
2008	The Dark Knight
2009	Avatar •
2010	Toy Story 3
2011	Harry Potter and the Deathly Hallows: Part II
2012	The Avengers •
2013	Frozen
2014	Transformers: Age of Extinction
2015	Star Wars Ep. VII: The Force Awakens •
2016	Captain America: Civil War
2017	Star Wars Ep. VIII: The Last Jedi
2018	Avengers: Infinity War •

VS

Sequel?

4% | **72%**

Critical score

TOP

MOONLIGHT **98%** | **98%** TOY STORY 3

BOTTOM

FORREST GUMP **72%** | **18%** TRANSFORMERS: AGE OF EXTINCTION

AVERAGE

★**88%** | **77%**★

Return on investment

TOP

MOONLIGHT **4,250%** | SHREK 2 **1,239%**

BOTTOM

BRAVEHEART **190%** | ARMAGEDDON **296%**

AVERAGE

$$$$$ **758%** | $$$$$ **558%**

Star player

Colin Firth **3 FILMS** ★★★ | Warwick Davis **6 FILMS** ★★★★★★

Tue 22nd JAN 2019

The Oscars vs the people

How does the taste of the Oscars' jury differ from that of the regular moviegoer? As this year's Academy Award nominations were announced, we pitted the Best Picture winners of the last 25 years against the best performing films at the global box office to see how they differ on plot, profit and on-screen violence

● WORDS: MARCUS WEBB ● ILLUSTRATION: CHRISTIAN TATE

How it works: We took the last 25 Best Picture winners at the Academy Awards and the top film at the worldwide box office the same year (via thenumbers.com). We then compared plot, genre, sequel status and cast (via IMDB.com), critical score (via rottentomatoes.com) and whether they have higher ratings for 'violence and scariness' or 'sexy stuff' (via commonsensemedia.com). We calculated return on investment by comparing box office return as a percentage of estimated production budget (via thenumbers.com).

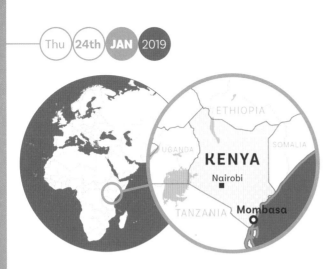

"This is not a lesser life"

On the outskirts of Nairobi sits Kibera, widely believed to be the largest urban slum in Africa. As a new project is launched to move its residents into more permanent housing, photographer **Brian Otieno**, who was born and raised in Kibera, provides a glimpse into life in this city of mud bricks and corrugated metal

● INTERVIEW: MARCUS WEBB ● PHOTOGRAPHY: BRIAN OTIENO

"Kibera is full of life – but nobody can quite agree on how full," says Brian Otieno, a photojournalist born in the sprawling, 2.5km-square settlement dubbed "Africa's largest slum". "The government puts the population at 180,000, but nobody here believes that number is anywhere near high enough. Some NGOs say there are two million living here, but I think that's too high. The fact is nobody really knows."

Whatever the number, there are plans afoot to decrease it. On 24th January the United Nations Office for Project Services (UNOPS) launched an ambitious $647 million project to create affordable and sustainable homes in Kenya. The plan is to move people out of the sort of mud-brick houses that dominate Kibera into more permanent housing.

Otieno has his doubts about whether the scheme will work. "We've seen the start of so many projects like this, but so many

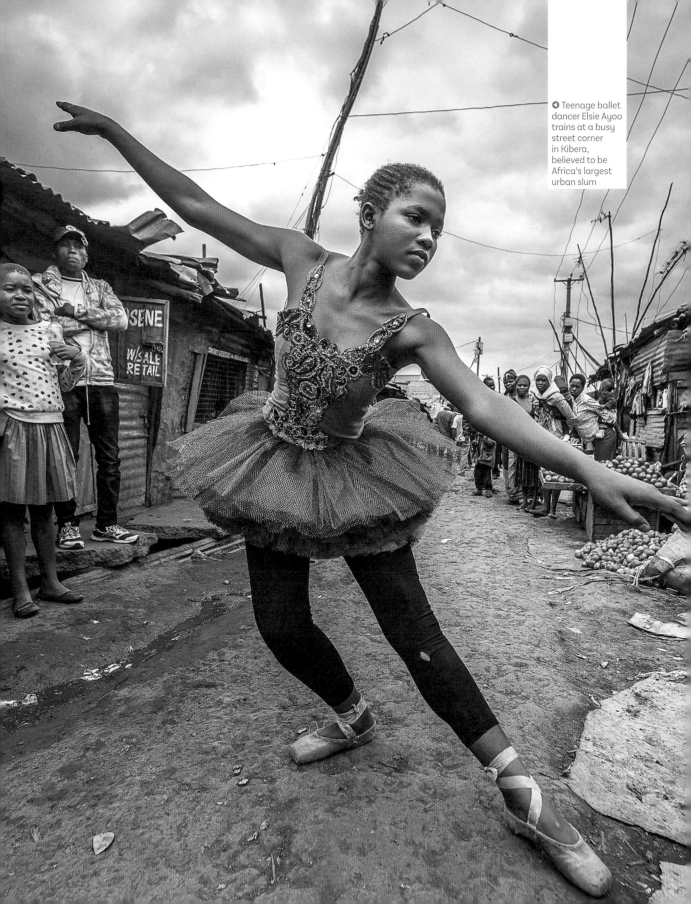

of them end up stalling," he says. "There was a government scheme recently to move people from near the railway tracks that run through Kibera into housing blocks. Some of the people who were relocated lasted just a few weeks before renting out their new houses and moving back to the slum. They are used to slum life."

Otieno has been documenting the realities of this "slum life" since 2014, after becoming frustrated with seeing the neighbourhood he was raised in only ever being portrayed as squalid and chaotic. The reality, he says, is very different. "I was tired of seeing my home depicted as an urban jungle with no potential," he says. "People here are trying to make something good with what they have. They have jobs, they run their own businesses. Poverty is a problem, crime is a problem – as it is everywhere. But this is not a lesser life."

Nairobi was founded in 1899 as a railway depot and by 1905 it had grown to replace Mombasa as the capital of British colonial Kenya. As it expanded, migrant African labourers were forced to live in the surrounding forest, far from the city centre, which was reserved for white settlers. The largest of the migrant camps was Kibera, which mostly sits on government land that can be reclaimed at any time – and tensions between Kiberans and the government remain high.

In 2018, 2,000 families were forcibly evicted to make room for a new road. "The people don't feel supported by the government at all," says Otieno. "It evicted people to make this road, demolished their houses and never gave compensation. They were just expected to move on and start again." Not only that, but, given that very few Kiberans own cars, the road is of little use to them.

Otieno believes that the government's priority should be improving the area's crumbling infrastructure. Electricity mostly comes from improvised hookups - in which the main power lines are illegally tapped - which are dangerous and lead to frequent blackouts. The lack of sanitation means there is an average of one toilet to every 500 people. This picture of disadvantage is set against a backdrop of a booming Kenyan economy. Between 2000 and 2017 the country's GDP quadrupled to $75 billion, but in that same period the number of people in severe poverty increased by ten percent.

The frustration at the widening gap between rich and poor is compounded by the fact that new developments often don't result in new jobs for locals. "A lot of these projects are created with the Chinese government, which is investing heavily in Kenya," says Otieno. "As a result the manual labourers tend to be Chinese, not Kenyans."

The employment rate in Kibera is estimated to be around 50 percent, with most workers taking the daily commuter train into Nairobi, 20 minutes away, where they work in low-paid jobs in the industrial area. "The train is the lifeline in many ways," says Otieno. "But it only runs twice a day, once into Nairobi in the morning and then back in the evening. From 7am the platform is full of people."

❮ Men peer out from the daily commuter train which passes through Kibera carrying passengers to and from Nairobi city centre

⊙ Filmmaker, designer, photographer and model Stephen Okoth, 25, walks through Kibera
⊙ Contenders and crowds at the annual Kentrack boxing tournament in Kibera, 29th July 2018

While Kibera's poverty is frequently reported, Otieno believes that this is only part of the story. Vibrant creative and sporting communities have emerged from Kibera's young population – and it is towards this talent that he wants to turn his lens. "I interact with a lot of artists, musicians, people who are trying to do something to make their lives better," says Otieno. "I've photographed filmmakers, fashion designers, boxers, footballers and poets in Kibera. Incredibly talented people looking for their break."

One of those opportunities comes in the form of the annual Mr and Miss Kibera competition. The annual event started as a beauty pageant, but has developed to celebrate sport and art and to develop leadership skills among young Kiberans. "It's difficult to explain how much of a big deal the competition is," says Otieno. "If you are selected as Mr or Miss Kibera you will get a lot of opportunities. You become a role model and get invited to things within the community. Sometimes they get employed by NGOs; it opens a lot of doors."

◔ Actors from Kibera promote a music video directed by Stephen Okoth (pictured opposite), who also created the costumes ◔ Contestants in the annual Mr and Miss Kibera pageant, 5th December 2017

○ Pupils playing at Toi Primary, one of Kibera's many schools and educational centres
◐ Children walk to school along the railway line in Kibera – according to the World Bank, Kenya has the third-highest literacy level in Africa

One of Otieno's favourite subjects to shoot is Elsie Ayoo (see p33). "She is a 17-year-old girl who's determined to become a professional ballet dancer," he says. "She is betting everything on making it. She has performed in theatres in Nairobi as a prima ballerina and her goal is to use dance to improve her life. I think she is on the right track."

"For most people, education is the most likely route out of extreme poverty," says Otieno. "You have to get educated, but all the public schools are overcrowded." Olympic Primary, one of Kibera's largest schools, has over 4,000 students. It once ranked among the top schools in Kenya, but an increasing intake over the past decade has seen its performance slide.

As children reach secondary-school age there has traditionally been pressure to drop out of education and start earning, but things are changing. "Most children in Kibera now receive a secondary education, but only thanks to NGOs and charities," says Otieno. "The school fees, while subsidised by the government, are too high for most people living in the area to pay without help. Secondary school is the final stop for most people – university is very expensive – but a secondary education means you can train to be an electrician, a mechanic, a sales agent or a secretary. It opens up new careers for people."

○ The remains of Toi Market after a devastating fire, March 2019
○ One of Toi Market's 5,000-plus traders surveys the damage

At the heart of Kibera is Toi Market, home to over 5,000 traders who deal in everything the locals need. Disaster struck on 12th March 2019 when a fire destroyed the entire market. "So many people lost everything," says Otieno. "People didn't have time to salvage their stock. The fire started at night, and by the morning everything was gone. But the people of Kibera are so resilient. A day later they started building the market up again. If you don't come to your space every day, you'll find somebody else has taken it. So you'd find guys that were selling clothes before the fire were now selling groceries. Then, when they'd made enough to buy clothes again, you'd see those reappearing. By May the market was up and running as if nothing had happened. This is Kibera – we find a way to carry on." ⑮

NOTES

In numbers

The United Nations defines a person as living in a slum if their household has at least one of the following four characteristics:

- Lack of access to improved drinking water
- Lack of access to improved sanitation
- Overcrowding (three or more persons per room)
- Dwellings made of non-durable material

The numbers are falling at an encouraging rate:

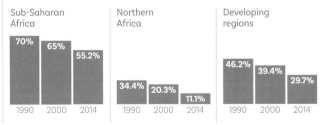

Proportion of urban population living in slums:

Sub-Saharan Africa
70% (1990) · 65% (2000) · 55.2% (2014)

Northern Africa
34.4% (1990) · 20.3% (2000) · 11.1% (2014)

Developing regions
46.2% (1990) · 39.4% (2000) · 29.7% (2014)

The movie matrix

January's film releases in order of critical reception and box office success

● WORDS AND RESEARCH: MARCUS WEBB

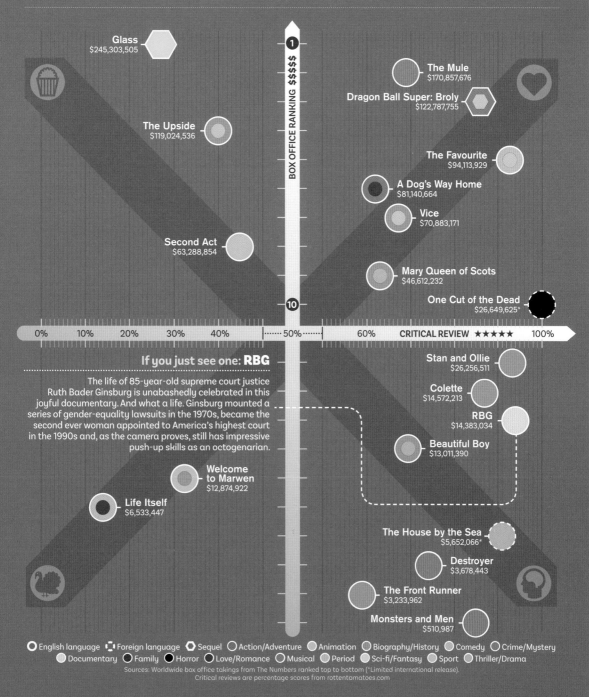

Glass $245,303,505

The Mule $170,857,676

Dragon Ball Super: Broly $122,787,755

The Upside $119,024,536

The Favourite $94,113,929

A Dog's Way Home $81,140,664

Vice $70,883,171

Second Act $63,288,854

Mary Queen of Scots $46,612,232

One Cut of the Dead $26,649,625*

BOX OFFICE RANKING $$$$$

1

10

0% 10% 20% 30% 40% 50% 60% **CRITICAL REVIEW** ★★★★★ 100%

Stan and Ollie $26,256,511

Colette $14,572,213

RBG $14,383,034

Beautiful Boy $13,011,390

If you just see one: RBG

The life of 85-year-old supreme court justice Ruth Bader Ginsburg is unabashedly celebrated in this joyful documentary. And what a life. Ginsburg mounted a series of gender-equality lawsuits in the 1970s, became the second ever woman appointed to America's highest court in the 1990s and, as the camera proves, still has impressive push-up skills as an octogenarian.

Welcome to Marwen $12,874,922

Life Itself $6,533,447

The House by the Sea $5,652,066*

Destroyer $3,678,443

The Front Runner $3,233,962

Monsters and Men $510,987

○ English language ⬚ Foreign language ◎ Sequel ○ Action/Adventure ◉ Animation ◉ Biography/History ◎ Comedy ○ Crime/Mystery
◉ Documentary ◉ Family ● Horror ◎ Love/Romance ○ Musical ◉ Period ◉ Sci-fi/Fantasy ◎ Sport ◎ Thriller/Drama

Sources: Worldwide box office takings from The Numbers ranked top to bottom (*Limited international release).
Critical reviews are percentage scores from rottentomatoes.com

FEB

Almanac

The month's news in brief

● EDITED BY: MATTHEW LEE

 The story behind the shot

Three former Tory MPs, Heidi Allen, Sarah Wollaston and Anna Soubry, pose for photos in London on 20th February after joining eight former Labour MPs as members of the recently established Independent Group. After a poor showing in May's EU elections, the new centrist party, now known as Change UK, sees six of its MPs leave, including Allen and Wollaston. Soubry becomes the new party leader.

Leon Neal/Getty Images

Fri · 1st

US ◎ The Trump administration announces the suspension of a major Cold War-era nuclear arms control treaty with Russia, claiming that Moscow has violated the agreement. The next day Russia also withdraws from the 1987 Intermediate-Range Nuclear Forces Treaty, which banned nuclear and non-nuclear missiles with short and medium ranges.

Sat · 2nd

HONG KONG ◎ A World War I-era German grenade is found in a shipment of potatoes. The grenade had been accidentally shipped to a Hong Kong crisp factory by suppliers in France.

Sun · 3rd

UK ◎ Police find the wreckage of a crashed plane in the English Channel. It is later confirmed that a body recovered from the wreckage is that of Emiliano Sala, the Argentine Cardiff City footballer who went missing on 21st January.

US ◎ The New England Patriots win the Super Bowl by beating the Los Angeles Rams in Atlanta. The 13-3 victory is the lowest-scoring Super Bowl in history.

Mon · 4th

VENEZUELA ◎ Several European nations including the UK, France and Germany join the US in recognising Juan Guaidó as Venezuela's interim president. Other European countries, including Greece and Italy, are unwilling to publicly oppose authoritarian leader Nicolás Maduro, who also retains the support of Russia and China.

US ◎ Liam Neeson reveals that, many years ago, he considered arbitrarily killing a black man in the street after a female acquaintance told him she was raped by a black person. Although the Northern Irish actor tells *The Independent* he is ashamed that he once harboured this impulse, his remarks are widely condemned. On 29th March, he apologises for making "hurtful and divisive" comments.

Tue · 5th

UK ◎ The Home Office says it believes that Isis hostage John Cantlie is still alive more than six years after being kidnapped. The British journalist, who was captured with US reporter James Foley in Syria in 2012, featured in a series of propaganda videos for the Islamist group but hasn't been seen since 2016. Foley was killed in 2014.

RUSSIA ◎ Talks begin in Moscow between the Taliban and senior Afghan officials with the aim of ending the 18-year war in Afghanistan.

 P048
'A law unto herself'

🕐 Many happy returns

A clutch of reports emerged in February about animals that had been spotted in the wild for the first time in years: this is how long had they managed to go incognito

Arabian caracal
Seen in Abu Dhabi after...
35 years

Wallace's giant bee aka 'the Flying Bulldog'
Seen in Indonesia after...
38 years

Tengmalm's owl
Seen in Shetland after...
107 years

An adult female **Fernandina giant tortoise**
Seen in the Galápagos National Park after...
110 years

Wed 6th

US ◗ **Nasa announces that 2018 was the fourth-warmest year on record.** Eighteen of the 19 warmest years since the US began keeping records nearly 140 years ago have occurred since 2001.

BELGIUM ◗ **Donald Tusk says there is a "special place in hell" for UK politicians who "promoted Brexit without even a sketch of a plan of how to carry it out safely".** The remarks made at a joint news conference with Irish leader Leo Varadkar are criticised by pro-Brexit politicians including Nigel Farage and Jacob Rees-Mogg.

Thu 7th

UK ◗ **The aphorism "beer before wine and you'll feel fine; wine before beer and you'll feel queer" is debunked by scientists.** The British and German researchers discovered that the severity of hangovers is not affected by the order in which drinks are consumed.

Fri 8th

UK ◗ **The Conservative minister who caused outrage by blocking an upskirting bill in June 2018 blocks an anti-FGM bill.** Sir Christopher Chope, who blocked new laws to protect children from female genital mutilation, insists that he objects on a point of principle when he believes bills are being rushed through without proper debate and says that he doesn't necessarily object to their substance.

Sat 9th

UK ◗ **A chimpanzee briefly escapes from its enclosure at Belfast Zoo, startling visitors.** The incident, which ends when the primate makes its way back to its pen a few minutes later, comes two weeks after a red panda cub escaped from the same zoo and was found in a nearby garden.

UK ◗ **A controversial 'no-deal' Brexit ferry contract with a company with no ships is cancelled by the government.** The £13.8m deal with Seaborne Freight, which attracted widespread criticism following the discovery that the company has never run a ferry service, collapses after Irish firm Arklow Shipping, which had secretly backed Seaborne, withdrew from the deal. On 28th March it's revealed that no Department of Transport officials had face-to-face meetings with either Seaborne or Arklow.

ITALY ◗ **Senior government officials voice their disapproval of the winning song at the Sanremo song festival, which will now be the Italian entry in the Eurovision Song Contest in Israel in May.** Deputy prime minister Matteo Salvini says 'Soldi' by Alessandro Mahmoud, whose father is Egyptian, was not the "most beautiful Italian song" in the contest, while prime minister Luigi Di Maio of the Five Star Movement says the contest jury represented "elites" and "radicals". The government has pushed for tough policies on immigration.

Sun 10th

US ◗ **Kacey Musgraves and Childish Gambino win the Best Album and Best Record awards** respectively at the Grammys.

HUNGARY ◗ **Viktor Orbán scraps income tax for women with four or more children in a move designed to encourage a baby boom.** The prime minister says he wants to reverse population decline while maintaining his hardline immigration policies.

Mon 11th

SRI LANKA ◗ **The government advertises for hangmen with "strong moral character" in state-run newspapers.** Although the country hasn't executed anybody since 1976, President Maithripala Sirisena has said he wants to execute drug traffickers. Sri Lanka hasn't had a hangman since 2014, when a newly hired executioner resigned in shock at his first sight of the gallows.

🕐 Record breakers

54
Most watermelons chopped on the stomach on a bed of nails in one minute
Sun 3rd
KV Saidalavi and Muhammad Ajsal KV, Anakkara, India

5.48km
Furthest swim wearing handcuffs
Wed 6th
Elham Sadat Asghari, Tehran, Iran

5.40m
Diameter of largest hula hoop spun
Tue 19th
Yuya Yamada, Yokohama, Japan

🧺 The basket case

In February the UK, France, Germany and Spain recognised Juan Guaidó as interim president of Venezuela against a backdrop of hyperinflation and economic collapse in the country. Regular hikes to the minimum wage by president Nicolás Maduro have not kept pace with soaring food prices and even with government food parcel programmes, life for ordinary Venezuelans has become almost impossible. Here's how things have changed since 2015

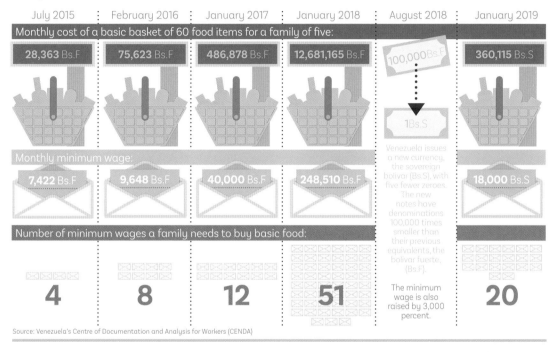

	July 2015	February 2016	January 2017	January 2018	August 2018	January 2019
Monthly cost of a basic basket of 60 food items for a family of five:	28,363 Bs.F	75,623 Bs.F	486,878 Bs.F	12,681,165 Bs.F	100,000 Bs.F → 1 Bs.S	360,115 Bs.S
Monthly minimum wage:	7,422 Bs.F	9,648 Bs.F	40,000 Bs.F	248,510 Bs.F		18,000 Bs.S
Number of minimum wages a family needs to buy basic food:	4	8	12	51		20

Venezuela issues a new currency, the sovereign bolivar (Bs.S), with five fewer zeroes. The new notes have denominations 100,000 times smaller than their previous equivalents, the bolivar fuerte, (Bs.F). The minimum wage is also raised by 3,000 percent.

Source: Venezuela's Centre of Documentation and Analysis for Workers (CENDA)

THAILAND ◎ An attempt by the sister of the king to become prime minister ends when the country's electoral commission bars Princess Ubolratana Rajakanya Sirivadhana Barnavadi's candidacy. The commission appears to have followed the guidance of King Maha Vajiralongkorn, whose response to her nomination by the populist Thai Raksa Chart party, which has links to exiled ex-leader Thaksin Shinawatra, was to insist that royalty was "above politics".

 Tue 12th

US ◎ Mexican cartel boss Joaquín 'El Chapo' Guzmán is found guilty on ten counts of drug trafficking in a trial in New York.

▣▣▶ P054
'Moment that mattered'

UAE ◎ A British football fan who says he was arrested for wearing a Qatar shirt in Abu Dhabi is released from a prison in Sharjah in the UAE. Ali Issa Ahmad claims he was detained after wearing the offending shirt at an Asian Cup match between Qatar and Iraq on 22nd January, and that security forces cut him with a knife, badly beat him and deprived him of food and water for several days. The UAE, which is in a diplomatic dispute with Qatar, insists Ahmad was detained for making a false claim and that his injuries were self-inflicted.

SPAIN ◎ The trial of 12 Catalan separatists begins in Madrid. The defendants, who were members of Catalonia's regional parliament, face charges of rebellion and misuse of public funds in relation to the staging of an October 2017 independence referendum without permission from Madrid and the unilateral declaration of independence a few weeks later.

GERMANY ◎ Two former Syrian intelligence officers who worked for Bashar al-Assad's security services early in the country's civil war are arrested for alleged crimes against humanity. A third man is detained in France as part of a joint investigation into former members of state security service the GID, which ran prisons in Syria in which regime critics were tortured.

 Wed 13th

SYRIA ◎ Shamima Begum, the only known survivor of three schoolgirls from east London who left the UK to join Isis in February 2015, is found at a Syrian refugee camp by a *Times* reporter. The 19-year-old, whose Dutch militant husband is being held in a Kurdish detention centre, says she lost two children to malnutrition while living in Isis-held territory. On 8th March the death of Begum's third child is confirmed.

 Thu 14th

INDIA ◎ A suicide car-bombing in the disputed region of Kashmir kills at least 46 Indian paramilitaries. Indian prime minister Narendra Modi warns that Pakistan will pay a "heavy price" for the attack on a military convoy, which is claimed by Pakistan-based militant group Jaish-e-Mohammed.

Famous for five minutes

Raphael Samuel, litigious anti-natalist

As parents of teenagers can attest, Raphael Samuel isn't the first to utter the words "I never asked to be born". But the 27-year-old Indian might be the first person to attempt to sue their parents for bringing them into the world. According to his 'anti-natalist' philosophy, life is pointless and the Earth would be improved if it didn't have dreadful humans draining its resources. Samuel's stunt may have helped his nihilistic memes spread on social media – to be picked up by global media in early February – but he might have messed with the wrong woman. Despite Samuel only suing "for a dollar or two", his mother reacted by jokingly telling her son that she will "destroy him" in court. The anti-natalist's oblivion may have got that little bit closer. The moral? Be careful what you wish for.

 (Fri) (15th)

UK ○ **Children around the country skip classes to campaign for action on climate change.**

◀▶ P058
'Desperate measures'

US ○ **Donald Trump declares a national emergency so he can bypass Congress and access funds to build a border wall**. The president's insistence that there is a national security emergency on the US-Mexico border is condemned by Democrats, who label it a "fake emergency" and argue that

Trump's declaration is an unconstitutional abuse of presidential power.

(Sat) (16th)

UK ○ **A House of Lords committee rules that by selling arms to Saudi Arabia during the Yemen conflict the government is breaking international humanitarian law**. The select committee's report calls for the government to suspend some export licenses.

UK ○ **Passengers are left stranded across Europe after airline BMI goes into administration** and cancels

Born

Green New Deal
Congressional resolution to tackle climate change introduced by a group of US Democratic lawmakers with the aim of achieving net-zero greenhouse gas emissions within ten years. Introduced **Thu 7th**

Onward
"Post-breakup concierge service" that helps newly single people in New York deal with the practical implications of starting afresh. Services include helping collect possessions from former shared homes. Launched **Thu 14th**

BritBox
Joint BBC/ITV streaming service designed to rival Netflix. Announced **Wed 27th**

Died

Albert Finney
British actor and star of *Tom Jones* and *Skyfall*, 82. **Thu 7th**

A380 superjumbo
Production on Airbus plane ceases due to lack of demand, after 12 years. Announced **Thu 14th**

André Previn
German-born US conductor and composer, best known for his scores for *My Fair Lady* and *Porgy and Bess*, 89. **Thu 28th**

all flights. BMI blames Brexit uncertainty and rising fuel costs.

(Sun) (17th)

History will judge us all"

UK ○ **Theresa May writes to Conservative MPs** to urge them to unite behind her Brexit deal. The prime minister says in the letter that she can persuade EU leaders to agree to changes to the Irish border 'backstop' plan disliked by many Tory members.

(Mon) (18th)

UK ○ **Seven MPs quit the Labour party to form 'The Independent Group', with some citing the party's anti-semitism controversy as their main reason for leaving**. An eighth Labour MP, Joan Ryan, joins the pro-EU group the next day.

(Tue) (19th)

UK ○ **The UK government moves to revoke Shamima Begum's citizenship.**

◀▶ P070
'Moment that mattered'

(Wed) (20th)

UKRAINE ○ **The country commemorates the fifth anniversary of the bloodiest day of the Kyiv protests against the government of Viktor Yanukovych.**

◀▶ P074
'The age of the ultras'

(Thu) (21st)

US ○ **An actor is arrested on suspicion of staging a racist and homophobic attack to advance his career**. Jussie Smollett, best known for his role in TV series *Empire*, claimed he was attacked in Chicago on 29th January by two masked men, but police concluded that their two

YouTube

Victory | Defeat

Wed 6th Poundland sells 20,000 £1 engagement rings in a week. The 'placeholder' rings are available in silver and gold.

Tue 12th Bahraini footballer Hakeem al-Araibi arrives home in Melbourne after 76 days in a Thai prison. The refugee was arrested in Bangkok during his honeymoon due to an extradition request by Bahrain relating to his alleged role in the 2011 Arab Spring revolts. Al-Araibi, who denies Bahrain's allegations, receives Australian citizenship in March.

Wed 20th Karl Lagerfeld's cat is set to inherit part of his $300m fortune after the fashion designer's death. Pets cannot directly inherit wealth in France so Choupette's money is likely to be held for it in a trust.

Thu 7th A **tempestuous Kuwaiti couple** is reported to have set a new record for the shortest marriage in the country's history. The pair broke up three minutes after tying the knot, when the husband mocked his new wife for tripping while turning to leave the courthouse and she asked the judge for an immediate annulment.

Sun 10th Fox News host Pete Hegseth is widely mocked after saying "germs are not a real thing" as he cannot see them, and that he hasn't washed his hands in ten years. He later insists his comments on *Fox & Friends* were a joke.

Sat 16th Paris's first restaurant for nudists closes after 15 months. O'naturel's sibling owners Stéphane and Mike Saada blame a lack of customers.

Mars vs Mercury

(A) **Wed 13th** Nasa confirms that its 15-year Opportunity mission to Mars is complete after failing to re-establish a connection with the roving robot
(B) **Sun 24th** Rami Malek wins the Academy Award for best actor for his portrayal of Queen frontman Freddie Mercury in *Bohemian Rhapsody*
Source: Google Trends, based on Google searches in February. Lines represent the popularity of each search term relative to the other on each day of the month.

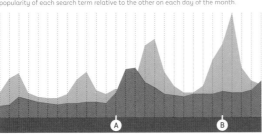

SAUL LOEB/AFP/Getty Images

---

main suspects had been hired by Smollett to help him stage the incident. Smollett, who maintains his innocence, has all charges against him dropped on 26th March.

JAPAN ○ **A Japanese spacecraft successfully lands on a speeding asteroid after a three-and-a-half-year journey from Earth.** The Hayabusa2 probe aims to collect rock samples from the surface of Ryugu so they can be studied by scientists.

Fri 22nd

SPAIN ○ **The North Korean embassy in Madrid is raided by ten people, who hold staff hostage for several hours before escaping with computers and hard drives.** In March a little-known activist group claims responsibility for the raid. Free Joseon describes itself as the North Korean provisional government in exile and says it aims to overthrow the Kim regime. In mid-April, US authorities arrest Christopher Ahn, a former US marine who is allegedly one of the Madrid embassy raiders.

Sat 23rd

US ○ **Paul Manafort is described as a "bold" criminal who "brazenly violated the law"** by prosecutors from special counsel Robert Mueller's office in a sentencing memo. The former Trump campaign chairman pleaded guilty in September 2018 to conspiracy against the US and faces up to 25 years in prison.

Sun 24th

US ○ **Green Book wins best picture** while Rami Malek and Olivia Colman win the respective awards for best actor and best actress at the Academy Awards in LA.

UK ○ **A Sunday Times investigation claims that five Britons are dying every day** due to opioid addiction.

The paper says the country is "in the grip of an opioid epidemic".

Mon 25th

NETHERLANDS ○ **A UN court in The Hague rules that Britain illegally took control of the Chagos Islands and they must be returned to Mauritius.** The ruling, which is not legally binding, states that the separation of the Indian Ocean archipelago from Mauritius in the 1960s was a "wrongful act".

Tue 26th

PAKISTAN ○ **India's military conducts airstrikes over the disputed Kashmiri border for the first time since the two countries were at war in 1971.** India says the bombings are "a pre-emptive" strike against terrorist training camps run by militant group Jaish-e-Mohammed. On Thursday 28th February, Pakistan offers to release captured Indian pilot Abhinandan Varthaman as a "peace gesture".

Wed 27th

VIETNAM ○ **A second summit between Donald Trump and Kim Jong-un convenes at a hotel in Hanoi.** Negotiations are cut short the following day after Kim's request that sanctions on North Korea be lifted.

Thu 28th

UK ○ **British Isis recruit Shamima Begum and her newborn baby are moved out of a Syrian refugee camp** due to concerns for their safety.

A law unto herself

Kimberley Motley is the only practising foreign defence lawyer in Afghanistan. As landmark peace talks begin between the Taliban and senior Afghan politicians and regional leaders – brokered by the Kremlin and hosted in Moscow – she tells **Marcus Webb** about defending justice in what is still a "country worth fighting for"

The elders had never experienced anything like it. They had gathered for a *jirga* – part of Afghanistan's informal justice system in which the leaders of a village convene to settle people's disputes – but rather than the usual all-male council there was a woman in the circle, and an American woman at that. What's more, she was leading proceedings. "They took a little bit of convincing," remembers Kimberley Motley, the woman in question – but the only practising foreign defence lawyer in Afghanistan is nothing if not persuasive.

The *jirga* was the second to meet to resolve the matter of an outstanding debt between Taj Mohammed and his neighbour. In 2014 Mohammed had fled the fighting in the country's southern Helmand province and moved his wife and nine children to a refugee camp on the outskirts of Kabul. When his wife and one of his sons fell ill, Mohammed borrowed $2,500 for medical expenses from his neighbour. Neither his wife or child survived and he was left with a debt he was unable to pay

back. The initial *jirga* ruled that the only way to settle the debt was for Mohammed's daughter Naghma to marry the neighbour's 19-year-old son. She was six years old. It was a decision that, according to Motley, broke Taj's heart but delighted the groom-to-be. "He was super-excited to get this little girl," says Motley with disdain. "He'd say to Taj: 'You're wasting your time getting her an education – when she's with me she won't be in school any more.'"

Motley heard about the case and offered to represent Naghma. She managed not only to get the elders to hold the second *jirga*, but to let her preside over it. "We reversed everything," she says. "The debt was satisfied [on hearing of the case Virgin CEO Richard Branson contacted Motley and offered to pay what was due] and all parties agreed that what they did was illegal, that they would allow their daughters to marry who they want to and that their children have the right to education." It was an incredible result orchestrated by Motley, although Naghma's gratitude was short lived. "She's actually a little mad at me," says Motley with a

◀ Kimberley Motley in Darul Aman Palace in western Kabul, December 2018

Motley shops in Kabul's Mandawi bazaar, March 2019

laugh. "A few months ago, she needed to have her tonsils out and it was me who took her to the doctor. She was really cross because they don't give you ice cream, like I said they do in America. She's probably over it now."

Sitting on *jirgas*, citing the Afghan constitution, dealing with the ire of sore-throated would-be child brides: it wasn't supposed to be like this. Motley was only in Afghanistan for the money. In 2008 she was a former beauty pageant winner-turned-lawyer working in the public defender's office in Milwaukee, Wisconsin. The pay wasn't great and Motley found herself approaching 30 with student loans to pay off and a young family to support. So when the offer came in to join a Department of Justice-funded programme to train defence attorneys in Afghanistan, she took it. "They were going to more than triple my salary. I had three kids, so I thought 'Fuck it, why not?'" she says. "I expected to go there for a year, make some money, come home." That was 11 years ago.

Before leaving for Afghanistan Motley had to complete a cultural sensitivity course in the US. "That training was just ridiculous," she says. "The tutors were solely white American men – there were no Afghans. We were taught that a woman is not supposed to shake the hands of a man, that a woman shouldn't even make eye contact, that you have to wear a headscarf at all times. The reality wasn't like that at all."

With the course complete, Motley left US soil for the first time and headed to Kabul. "I was there to train these people who've been practising law in the country for over ten years in how they could be better Afghan lawyers, after having been in the country for a week and with no experience of their justice system. I just thought that was so absurd," she says. "I was just turning up and reading from a binder and so I thought, 'I want to start educating myself on what this legal system actually is.'"

Eager to learn more, she asked her supervisor when they would be visiting a court and was surprised to learn that in the four years the programme had been running not one of the trainers had ever been to see a trial. They'd barely left the hotel where the training was conducted. Motley soon rectified that, sitting in on a three-judge tribunal at the national security court. "They brought in this elderly man with a bag over his head and shackles on his arms and his legs," she remembers. "He looked more like a hostage than a defendant. I was thinking, 'This is not cool.'"

The defendant, who didn't have a lawyer present, was a taxi driver who had been stopped by police for carrying a group of men with guns. He said they were strangers who had got into his taxi but the prosecution claimed they were associates and that he was a terrorist. "The first thing the accused said was, 'If I'm a terrorist, bring the guy before me who accused me of being a terrorist,' not realising he was invoking his legal right to confrontation," says Motley. "The judge ignored this and pointed out that the man had signed a confession. The guy replied with: 'They beat me to sign that confession.' He was trying to show his bruises and the judge pounded on his table, and said, 'Enough! Don't disrupt me.' That's how they translated it. Five minutes later they convicted him of being a terrorist. I believe he got eight years."

Motley was shocked at the lack of process, the lack of evidence and the lack of a defence lawyer, to which the accused was legally entitled. "I was a month and a half into [my time in] the country and I just felt sick," she says. After the hearing, Motley approached the judge to raise her concerns. "I asked 'Why was he found guilty?' And the judge's answer was basically 'He was found guilty because he's guilty.' It felt like the judges thought that I, as an American, should be happy that they were being tough on terror."

> **"**
> They were going to more than triple my salary. I had three kids, so I thought 'why not?'
> **"**

Determined to see every aspect of the legal system, Motley's next stop was the prisons. "I visited Pul-e-Charkhi, the largest prison in Afghanistan," she says. "It didn't really cross my mind that there were English-speaking foreigners locked up in Afghan prisons, but I found them there." A number of the inmates had written letters detailing their cases and how they felt wronged by the justice system. When Motley approached them they tried to give her the letters. Initially she refused. "I didn't want to get into trouble," she says. "And then I remember one guy looking at me and saying, 'Please help us, no one is helping.' And I was like, 'Shit'. So I snatched the letters, and stuffed them in my backpack."

The combination of what she read in the letters and her experience in the courts made Motley feel that she could do more in Afghanistan than read from a binder in a conference room. "It got my wheels turning," she recalls. "I thought, 'Maybe I can help them.' I didn't even think about it as a business at that point in time. I just wanted to help them because it seemed wrong."

She returned to the prison and emerged with two of the letter writers – Bevan Campbell and Anthony Malone – as clients. Soon she was the only foreigner with a licence to litigate in Afghanistan's courts. Both Campbell and Malone had chequered pasts, but Motley

Kiana Hayeri

argued that this did not affect their right to a fair trial. Campbell, a former major in the South African air force turned Afghan security contractor, had been sentenced to 16 years for allegedly smuggling six kilos of heroin through Kabul airport – he maintained that he believed it was protein powder that had been given to him by a friend. Malone, meanwhile, a former British paratrooper accused of kidnap and torture offences in the UK, fled to Afghanistan where he was later jailed for owing local businessmen money. Motley quickly educated herself on the details of Afghan law – she likens the process of digging up useful local laws to archaeology – and secured the release of both men. Campbell was released having served six years. Malone returned to the UK where he was sentenced to eight years for his earlier offences.

After finishing her obligations to the training organisation, rather than returning home Motley set up her practice in Kabul. "Everyone – apart from my family – said, 'You shouldn't be doing this. You don't know what you're doing,'" she says. Motley remained determined. "It seemed that I had a real responsibility. Why go to law school if I'm not going to allow myself to be in this situation?" She argues that it was her first clients who were taking the real risk. "It's a big gamble to go with a non-Afghan lawyer, let alone an American woman, representing you when your liberty is at stake. If it didn't work out for me then I could just get a plane ticket and leave. They didn't have that option."

Motley's wins kept coming – she cites a 90 percent success rate – and she soon had a wide range of clients, from multinational companies, who she charges, to Afghan women accused of moral crimes and children such as Naghma, whose cases she mostly takes pro bono. In her 11 years practising in Afghanistan Motley has assisted in the return of two Australian children taken to the country illegally by their father, helped a 12-year-old child bride successfully take her abusive husband and in-laws to the supreme court and secured a presidential pardon for a rape victim who was sentenced for adultery, the first pardon for a so-called morality crime in the country.

These successes, built in part on Motley's ability to cite Sharia law and arcane aspects of the Koran in defence of her clients, have not come without their fair share of danger. Motley has had a grenade thrown into her office, which failed to explode. She tells a story of how she spent a prison riot trapped in a security hut watching *Sesame Street*. She was also in the Serena Hotel when it was raided by Taliban gunmen in March 2014, an attack that left nine people dead. The incident shook Motley and she now lives and works out of an undisclosed location. "Only a handful of people know where I live," she says. "Not because I don't trust them, but because anyone can be compromised." Despite the separation and the security risks, Motley feels at home in Afghanistan. "I think I am a lot more comfortable in Kabul than most people would be because I grew up in the projects, in a bad neighbourhood, so I have this innate street sense," she says.

In recent years Motley's client list has expanded. She has represented defendants in Bolivia, as well as Malaysia's former deputy prime minister, Anwar Ibrahim, and Cuban dissident artist Danilo Maldonado – a case that saw her arrested when she attempted to hold a press conference outside the National Capitol building in Havana. She keeps coming back to Afghanistan, however, and her latest case could be her biggest to date.

○ Motley sitting on the jirga discussing the fate of Naghma Mohammad

> " They agreed that their daughters could marry who they want to and that all children have the right to an education "

Fawzia Koofi is one of Afghanistan's most prominent female MPs and women's rights activists. Elected to office in 2005, she became the country's first female deputy speaker. In August 2018, two months before Koofi was to seek a widely predicted re-election, the electoral complaints commission disqualified her from standing, accusing her of links to a private armed militia and of possessing illegal weapons. Koofi strenuously denies the charges and Motley has taken the case to clear her name.

"When you're a popular woman, they try to crucify you," she says. "The electoral commission have nothing to substantiate their claims." Motley has launched criminal charges against three people within the commission and is attempting to get Koofi's status reinstated before her successor is sworn in – a process that is being delayed while accusations of corruption during the October 2018 election are being investigated. The stakes couldn't be higher. "As a member of parliament, you are provided with security by the government. Once they take her security away, she and her daughter are a lot more exposed," says

○ Afghanistan's first female deputy speaker, Fawzia Koofi (centre) in Kabul ahead of the 2014 elections. Koofi says she has been falsely accused of links to a private armed militia. She is being defended by Kimberley Motley

Motley. "I fear her being assassinated, frankly." Koofi has not let the case hold her back. In February 2019 she joined peace talks with the Taliban in Moscow. As the only female present she was determined to ensure that women's rights were not discarded during negotiations.

Motley sees the treatment of Koofi as a worrying sign that Afghanistan still has a long way to go. The country is in a perilous position. President Trump has been vocal about his desire to withdraw remaining US troops in the near future. Meanwhile there are two competing tracks of peace talks: Russia and the US are backing separate negotiations with different stakeholders. Both include the Taliban but, so far, exclude the Afghan government, which the Taliban has refused to meet. "I think some

things are headed in the wrong direction," says Motley. "But I am optimistic. I've seen a lot of people do amazing things in Afghanistan. There are a lot of smart and strong people here that love their country and want to fight for it, and I do think it's a country worth fighting for. It's a country worth protecting. The fact that Afghanistan has allowed me, as a foreigner, to come in and practise law is incredible. They could've kicked me out of here years ago."

Until they do Motley continues her work. Refusing to wear a headscarf, asking for meetings with men, shaking them by the hand, looking them in the eye. It's as though she didn't listen to a single word her cultural sensitivity tutors said. ⓰

NOTES

In numbers

Nearly 18 years after George W Bush launched airstrikes targeting the Taliban and al-Qaeda in response to the 9/11 attacks, Afghanistan has become the US's longest military engagement. But how does it compare to other wars in terms of Americans killed in action?

World War II	Korean War	Vietnam War	Iraq War	Afghanistan
US involvement: 1941-1945	US involvement: 1950-1953	US involvement: 1964-1975	US involvement: 2003-2010	US involvement: 2001-
US fatalities: ↑291,557	US fatalities: ↑33,739	US fatalities: ↑47,434	US fatalities: ↑3,490	US fatalities: ↑1,833*
Monthly mortality rate: ↑6,626	Monthly mortality rate: ↑912	Monthly mortality rate: ↑389	Monthly mortality rate: ↑33	Monthly mortality rate: ↑9*
				*As of 25th June 2019

Moment that mattered

Joaquín 'El Chapo' Guzmán is found guilty

Laura Bonilla, AFP reporter ● INTERVIEW: MARCUS WEBB

"For three months the trial of Joaquín 'El Chapo' Guzmán – the world's most famous narco trafficker – was pretty much my whole life. I was in court every day and just getting in to the room was a drama. Space was limited, so journalists were sleeping on the street to make sure they got a spot, I was getting up at 4am every day to make sure I got in. The trial would last until 5pm and then I'd often be writing late into the evening.

"We'd be searched every day before entering the court and we'd have to surrender our phones. We weren't allowed to record any video, take pictures or make audio recordings. They couldn't risk anything leaking that could identify the jury members in case El Chapo's associates found out who they were and applied pressure on them to find him innocent. So it was old school journalism for three months – just you, your pen, your brain, and the most incredible story being recounted in front of you. It was overwhelming at times, there was so much evidence and so many witnesses – a parade of Guzmán's former associates, friends, enemies, lovers...

"One of the most memorable characters was Christian Rodriguez, the 'IT guy'. He was a 20-year-old Colombian university graduate running his own company when he was first hired to handle the IT security for Guzmán's Sinaloa cartel in Mexico. This is not a guy who was born into narco trafficking, this was a smart university student coming from a middle class family. He knew he was working with criminals but he wanted adventure, the money was good and they sent him all around the world. He was caught by the FBI in a sting operation in the US and started collaborating with them. So at 20-something he was working for one of the most powerful cartels in the world, while at the same time he was also informing on them to the American authorities. "We were told that El Chapo learned of this and tried to have him killed and he fled. He had a wife and child that he had to leave behind to start a new life in America under a hidden identity. Now he can't have any contact with them or ever talk about his past. The trial was full of stories like this – it was like a different movie plot every day, but it was all real.

"There was the big Colombian narco trafficker who had undergone so much plastic surgery to avoid detection that he looked grotesque. He was arrested in Brazil with his lover, a Brazilian bodybuilder, and is now in jail. When he was working with El Chapo he used to have several huge planes and he would ship the cocaine to Mexico and from there El Chapo would send it to the United States. The Colombian authorities confiscated more than a billion dollars from him. He told the jury he'd killed approximately 150 people, adding 'I didn't keep count' without a flicker of emotion. It was scary, it was surreal, it was fascinating.

"Most of the witnesses testified expecting to get a reduction on their sentence or better conditions in jail, but that depends on the judge, the prosecutors can't promise they'll get anything. It's a risky move. Even in prison El Chapo is a dangerous man and there's always the threat of retribution. It was horrific sometimes hearing about the violence his cartel inflicted. We heard descriptions of unimaginable torture being carried out.

"Guzmán was born poor and was desperate to get out of poverty. He never learned how to read or write very well, which we saw from text messages of his that appeared as evidence in the trial. But he was a natural businessman and throughout the 80s and 90s he rode the wave of the drug business, the most lucrative in Latin America. The US authorities estimated that he

"One witness told the jury he'd killed approximately 150 people, adding 'I didn't keep count'"

PGR/Prensa Internacional via ZUMA Wire

Joaquín 'El Chapo' Guzmán photographed during his extradition from Mexico to the US, 19th January 2017

sent something like 450 tonnes of cocaine, amphetamines and marijuana to the US over 25 years, amassing a personal fortune of 14 billion dollars. They hope to confiscate this, but so far they've failed to find a single dollar.

"Several of Guzmán's former associates testified that they had paid hundreds of millions of dollars in bribes to high-ranking government officials, legislators and bankers. We also heard that Guzmán himself lived like a king before his arrest. He had ranches in every state of Mexico, he had a private zoo with a train that would take him and his guests around. He had a yacht called 'Chapito', 'little Chapo'. He was flying all over the world. Witnesses at the trial said they accompanied him on gambling trips to Macau and to clinics in Europe where he received rejuvenation treatments.

"Guzmán was first arrested in Mexico in 2014, but escaped through a 1.5km tunnel under his jail cell. He was captured again in 2016 and extradited to the US. There's no doubt the arrest – and the trial - has been a big publicity coup for the DEA [Drug Enforcement Agency], and Guzmán is the biggest narco trafficker the US has ever put behind bars.

"However, I'm not sure it's going to result in a reduction in the amount of drugs being trafficked. In fact, the amount of drugs coming from Mexico to the US has gone up since Guzmán's arrest. The Sinaloa cartel split after Chapo's capture, but it is still alive. Part of the cartel is led by Guzmán's sons, part by Ismael El Mayo Zambada, who co-founded the cartel with Chapo and who is now around 70 years old. Unlike Chapo – a man who always courted fame and wants not only to have a movie made about his life, but to star in and direct it – Zambada stays hidden. He's never spent a day in jail. It doesn't matter if it's Chapo, Zambada or somebody else, as long as there are people who are ready to buy drugs there will be people capitalising on that demand and using violent methods to protect their business.

"We're seeing more and more people – from all classes – consuming drugs. According to the 2018 Congressional Research Service report, Mexican drug cartels take in between $19 billion and $29 billion annually from drug sales in the US. I think a lot of

people don't realise, or don't want to realise, all the violence and all the lives that are lost along the way to their party. The same report also says that in 2017 a record 29,000 people were murdered in Mexico. During the 2017-2018 election period 114 Mexican candidates and politicians were killed by crime bosses and others in an effort to intimidate public office holders.

"My colleague Javier Valdez, AFP's stringer in Sinaloa, was killed in the street in front of his office two years ago. He was a leading voice in the investigations against drug traffickers in Mexico and founded *Ríodoce*, a weekly magazine dedicated to the coverage of organized crime. He was murdered, presumably on the orders of members of the Sinaloa cartel.

"Despite the violence, there are people in Mexico who love Guzmán. El Chapo is this almost mythical figure. He has donated a lot of money to the poor people of Sinaloa state where the government has been pretty much absent. When he was captured people from Sinaloa were very worried, saying they felt unprotected now that El Chapo was in jail.

"You could see this devotion on show at the trial: I met one couple who even flew to New York to be there as a way of celebrating their wedding anniversary. There was a female priest who would pray for Chapo over a copy of the bible every day from five o'clock in the morning.

"On the day of the verdict I was sitting next to El Chapo's wife, Emma Coronel, another big character. She was a former beauty queen and would be in court almost every day of the trial, immaculately made-up, sitting a few metres from her husband. As the jury came in to deliver the verdict, she turned towards me and asked in Spanish, my mother tongue, what the English word is for 'guilty'.

"The jury found Guzmán guilty on all ten counts of drug trafficking. He didn't show a lot of emotion during the trial, but when the jury announced the verdict, he looked at Coronel, blew her a kiss and made a heart sign with his hands. She replied with the same gesture. It will be one of the last times she will ever see him, as the authorities don't let her visit him. It was yet another strange moment. I'd spent three months listening to some of the monstrous things this man has done, but it ended with him telling his wife he loved her." 🜚

○ Emma Coronel exits the court during the trial of her husband, Joaquín Guzmán

"

As the jury came in to deliver the verdict, Coronel turned towards me and asked what the English word is for 'guilty'

"

Spencer Platt/Getty Images

EU were always on my mind

As Theresa May's Brexit strategy fails to win the support of the House of Commons, we trace how quickly comments threads below unrelated online news stories turn to the debate about leaving the European Union

NEWS STORY   COMMENT NUMBER

A Belgian papillon wins best in show at Crufts

The Times, 11th March

1

"Bloody Brussels, now they are taking over our dog shows."

February heatwave sets British record

The Times, 25th February

2

"It's all the fault of Brexit"

Brits must limit meat intake to 'slash early deaths and save planet'

The Sun, 16th January

4

"They are not scientists they are REMOANER SCINOs [scientists in name only]."

***Only Fools and Horses: The Musical* makes its stage debut**

Guardian, 20th February

6

"If Del Boy was still alive today I think he would be horrified by the damage this Tory government has done to the country through things like Brexit and universal credit."

The first episode of *Danny Dyer's Right Royal Family* is broadcast

Guardian, 23rd January

11

"Arise Sir Danny, valiant foe of twats with their trotters up. History beckons. Save us from Brexit!"

China lands a probe on the far side of the moon

Financial Times, 3rd January

15

"We need to revoke Article 50 backed by a People's Vote..."

Man Utd knock PSG out of the Champions League

Telegraph, 7th March

18

"It was a penalty. It happened. Like Brexit. It's real"

Greggs release a vegan sausage roll

Mail Online, 3rd January

27

"Why is classic British cuisine being ruined by these left-wing remoaners? I imagine this is the kind of muck served up in the EU?"

World Cup winning goalkeeper Gordon Banks dies

Mail Online, 24th March

74

"As England's safest pair of hands, perhaps Gordon should have been in on Brexit negotiations?"

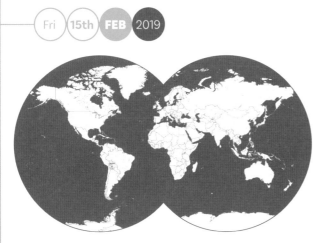

Desperate measures

On 15th February, 10,000 UK students went on 'strike', skipping school to protest for radical reductions in the country's CO_2 emissions. Two months later, activist group Extinction Rebellion occupied sites in London and demanded the government declare a 'climate emergency'. But what is the size of the UK's CO_2 problem – and what might it take to bring about the rapid decarbonisation of the country's economy? ● RESEARCH: JOE LO, ROB ORCHARD ● ILLUSTRATION: CHRISTIAN TATE

Sins of emission

The UK's CO_2 emissions have fallen significantly in recent years due to new environmental initiatives and the decline in heavy industry. However the country's per capita emissions are still higher than the global average.

Average annual CO_2 emissions per capita ⬚ 1990 ● 2017/2018
All figures quoted are in metric tons

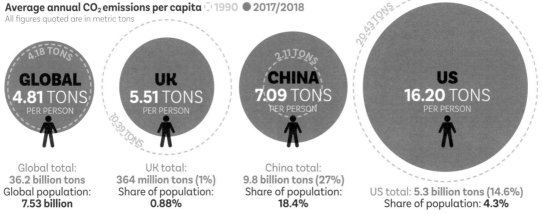

GLOBAL 4.18 TONS
4.81 TONS PER PERSON

Global total:
36.2 billion tons
Global population:
7.53 billion

UK 10.39 TONS
5.51 TONS PER PERSON

UK total:
364 million tons (1%)
Share of population:
0.88%

CHINA 2.11 TONS
7.09 TONS PER PERSON

China total:
9.8 billion tons (27%)
Share of population:
18.4%

US 20.43 TONS
16.20 TONS PER PERSON

US total: **5.3 billion tons (14.6%)**
Share of population: **4.3%**

Sources: Global Carbon Atlas, Global Carbon Project, Our World in Data, UK government, World Bank

Leon Neal/Getty Images

Students gather in London's Parliament Square during a climate protest on 15th February 2019

What if everyone in the UK went vegan?

Average annual amount of CO_2 emitted by production, transportation, storage, cooking and wastage of food:

For a British
MEAT-EATER
2.31
TONS PER PERSON

For a British
PESCATARIAN
1.61
TONS PER PERSON

For a British
VEGETARIAN
1.56
TONS PER PERSON

For a British
VEGAN
1.19
TONS PER PERSON

Source: 'Dietary greenhouse gas emissions of meat-eaters, fish-eaters, vegetarians and vegans in the UK' by Peter Scarborough

CO_2 saved per year:

3.2kg
CO_2 emitted producing one **beef burger**

1.2kg
CO_2 emitted producing one **vegan burger**
Based on ingredients in BBC Good Food recipes

65 million tons
If all 58,100,240 of the UK's **meat eaters** went vegan

1.1 million tons
If all 2,640,920 of the UK's pescatarians went vegan

1.5 million tons
If all 3,961,380 of the UK's vegetarians went vegan

Average annual CO_2 emissions per person in the UK **5.51** TONS

1.02 TONS PER PERSON SAVED

67.6 million tons
If everybody in the UK went vegan

Note: The vast majority of agricultural emissions are non-CO_2 and the CO_2 figures quoted in this section include the damage done by methane and nitrous oxide as a CO_2 equivalent. In this and subsequent infographics we've used the latest available figures from credible sources, but **these are estimates in many cases and should be taken as giving a broad overview rather than a forensic analysis**. The featured impacts of radical CO_2 decrease are limited to proximate effects for reasons of space and because broader effects are often unquantifiable and/or unforeseeable.

Sources: Department for Business (DBEIS), Department for Transport (DfT), the Vegan Society

That'll do, pig

If the UK went vegan overnight there would be significant numbers of surplus livestock and, when they died, lots of free land*

Current UK livestock populations:
4,648,000 PIGS
9,610,000 CATTLE AND CALVES (including 1,895,000 dairy cows)
33,781,000 SHEEP AND LAMBS
188,442,000 POULTRY

135,625 km²
Estimated UK land taken up for meat and dairy production:
an area the size of England
(only 6% of UK land is urban)

FOR THE CHOP?
Overnight mass veganism would deal a severe blow to the UK's meat and dairy economy

£8.2 billion Value of UK livestock industry

97,000 People employed in the UK meat industry

249 Red meat abattoirs in the UK

6,000 Butchers' shops in the UK

£8.8 billion Value of UK dairy industry

73,000 People employed in the UK dairy industry

13,815 Dairies in the UK

*Effects above are limited to the UK's own food industries, but the effect of British citizens all going vegan would have significant impact outside the country due to the country's high levels of food imports. Sources: Agriculture & Horticulture Development Board, Dairy UK, DEFRA, Greenpeace, House of Commons briefing paper, ONS

Oli Scarff/Getty Images

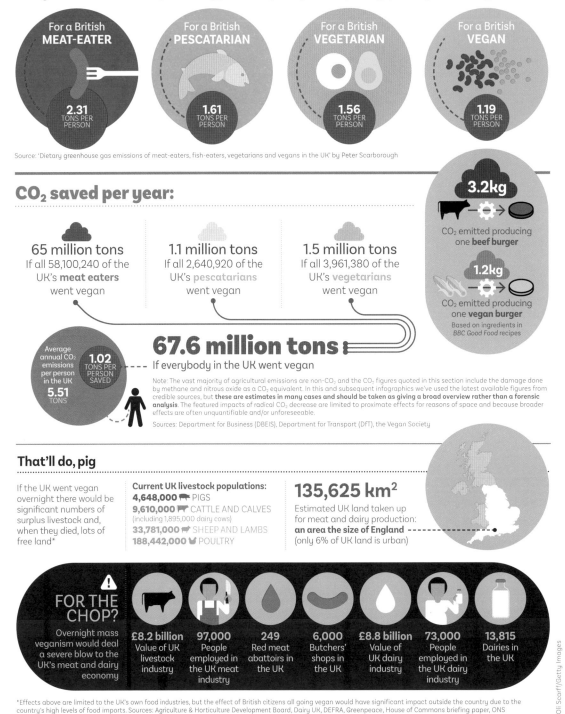

How is the UK doing?

There are signs that the UK is starting to fall out of love with meat – or at least some meat. The latest figures available from the UN Food and Agriculture Organization show that between 1989 and 2013, British per capita consumption per capita of beef fell by 16 percent and of lamb by 33 percent. Pork consumption increased, but only by two percent per capita. The exception is the UK's growing hunger for hen: poultry meat consumption grew by 80 percent over the same period to 32 kilos per person per year. This chicken spike means that Britons' total consumption of meat grew by 12 percent over the period to nearly 80 kilos per capita per year.

What if everyone stopped flying in and out of the UK?

2,230,000
Total number of flights landing at and taking off from UK airports each year:

- BUSINESS FLIGHTS = 19%
- HOLIDAYS = 44%
- **VISITING FRIENDS AND FAMILY = 35%**
- OTHER = 2%

CO₂ saved per year:

3 million tons
If all UK domestic flights ceased

13.3 million tons
If everyone stopped flying to or from the UK on business

24.5 million tons
If everyone stopped flying to or from the UK to visit friends and/or family

30.8 million tons
If everyone stopped flying to or from the UK on holiday

Average annual CO₂ emissions per person in the UK
5.51 TONS

1.10 TONS PER PERSON SAVED

73 million tons
If all flights to and from the UK ceased

Note: We have doubled the CO₂ figures for flying because the European Parliament estimates that the non-CO₂ effects of flying – including its impact on cloud formation, ozone generation and methane reduction mechanisms – double its contribution to climate change.

Sources: Department for Business (DBEIS), Department for Transport (DfT)

FLIGHT RISKS ⚠

230,000
Number of people employed in the aviation industry in the UK, including aircraft manufacturing and maintenance and air freight

£ **£22 billion**
Value of UK aviation industry

What if all the UK's cars were electric?

8.8 TONS of CO₂
Average emissions from building an electric car

281.6 million tons of CO₂ to replace the UK's 32 million cars

CO₂ saved per year:

69.7 million tons
After the initial 281.6 million ton spike in emissions and provided they run purely on electricity from renewable sources

+ 500,000 tons
From replacing motorbikes with bicycles
(• 0.0075 tons per person)

Source: DfT, Ricardo consultancy

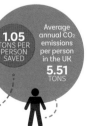

1.05 TONS PER PERSON SAVED

Average annual CO₂ emissions per person in the UK
5.51 TONS

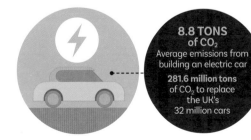

How is the UK doing?

Terribly. According to the UK's Department of Transport, the number of passengers flying in and out of British airports has increased by 187 percent since 1989 – and the country's skies are only set to get busier. If the plans for Heathrow's third runway submitted for public consultation on 18th June 2019 go ahead, the number of annual take-offs and landings into the UK's biggest airport, pictured, will increase by 59 percent from 476,000 in 2018 to 756,000 by 2050. Additional growth is set to begin even before the new runway opens: as part of its plans, Heathrow announced it will utilise "new navigation technology" to add up to ten extra take-offs and landings an hour. The current average is 74.

What if the UK closed all its fossil fuel power plants?

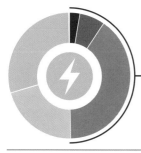

168,900,000,000 kWh (168.9tWh)
Annual energy production from UK power stations run on fossil fuels

● OIL + ● COAL + ● GAS = 50%

● RENEWABLE ENERGY SOURCES = 29.4%
● NUCLEAR ENERGY = 20.8%

Option 1: Swap fossil fuels for solar panels

3,000 kWh
Annual average energy produced by a south-facing 3.5 kw solar panel system in the UK

Average system size: 14.6m²

56,300,000
Number of 3.5 kw solar panel systems needed to replace energy produced by power stations run on fossil fuels

Total area needed: 822 km², about the size of Monmouthshire

£281.5 billion
Estimated cost of purchasing 56,300,000 3.5kw solar panel systems at £5,000 each

(does not include presumed bulk discount for buying 56.3 million units)

Option 2: Swap fossil fuels for wind turbines

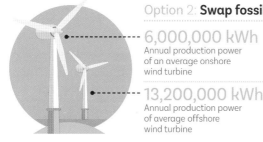

6,000,000 kWh
Annual production power of an average onshore wind turbine

28,150
Number of onshore wind turbines needed to replace fossil fuel energy production

13,200,000 kWh
Annual production power of average offshore wind turbine

12,795
Number of offshore wind turbines needed to replace fossil fuel energy production

£67.7 billion
Estimated cost of building 12,795 offshore turbines, based on the £1 billion cost of the UK's Walney Wind Farm, the world's largest offshore wind farm with 189 turbines

---

Option 3: Swap fossil fuels for nuclear reactors

☢☢☢☢☢☢☢☢☢☢☢☢☢☢☢ **15**
Current number of nuclear reactors in the UK, each producing an average of 4.69 twh of electricity per year

☢☢☢☢☢☢☢☢☢☢☢☢☢☢☢☢☢☢
☢☢☢☢☢☢☢☢☢☢☢☢☢☢☢☢☢☢ **36**
Number of new nuclear reactors needed to replace current fossil fuel energy production

£365.4 billion
Estimated cost of building 36 nuclear reactors, based on £20.3 billion cost of twin-reactor station Hinkley Point C, to be completed in 2025

CO_2 saved per year:

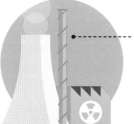

Average annual CO_2 emissions per person in the UK **5.51 TONS**

1.08 TONS PER PERSON SAVED

71.8 million tons
Current emissions from UK use of fossil fuels in power stations

⚙ Does not factor in the initial CO_2 costs of creation and installation of new solar/wind/nuclear facilities

📊 Analysis above does not take into account the fluctuations in energy supply caused by peaks and troughs in solar and wind production. In order to make a like for like swap, the vexed issue of energy storage would have to be solved.

Sources: BBC, BEIS, Centre for Alternative Technology, Eco Experts, Energy Sage, Nuclear AMRC, Wind Europe

Mike Hewitt/Getty Images

How is the UK doing?

The UK is well on the way to kicking its fossil fuel habit. It was recently announced that Fiddler's Ferry, one of only six coal-fired energy stations operational in the country, will close in March 2020. Meanwhile in February 2019 electricity was produced for the first time from Hornsea One, which will be the world's biggest offshore wind farm by 2020. In May 2019, a government-appointed enquiry began considering proposals for an 890-acre solar power plant in north Kent capable of powering more than 91,000 homes. In the last decade renewable energy has climbed from supplying just two percent of the UK's power to almost a third today.

What if the UK planted a lot more trees?

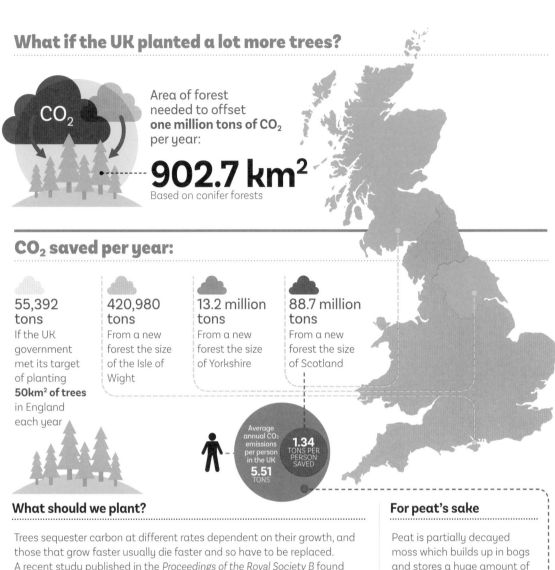

CO_2

Area of forest needed to offset **one million tons of CO_2** per year:

902.7 km^2
Based on conifer forests

CO_2 saved per year:

55,392 tons
If the UK government met its target of planting **50km^2 of trees** in England each year

420,980 tons
From a new forest the size of the Isle of Wight

13.2 million tons
From a new forest the size of Yorkshire

88.7 million tons
From a new forest the size of Scotland

Average annual CO_2 emissions per person in the UK
5.51 TONS

1.34 TONS PER PERSON SAVED

What should we plant?

Trees sequester carbon at different rates dependent on their growth, and those that grow faster usually die faster and so have to be replaced. A recent study published in the *Proceedings of the Royal Society B* found that forests planted with a variety of tree species are able to capture as much as twice as much carbon as monoculture plantations

Oak
Lifespan: **100 years**
Trees per hectare: **63**

1 TON OF CO_2 — 10 trees

Wild cherry
Lifespan: **45 years**
Trees per hectare: **92**

1 TON OF CO_2 — 8 trees

Poplar
Lifespan: **25 years**
Trees per hectare: **156**

1 TON OF CO_2 — 11 trees

For peat's sake

Peat is partially decayed moss which builds up in bogs and stores a huge amount of carbon. Around 80 percent of the UK's peatbogs have been damaged by drainage, burning and overgrazing. If we reverse this damage we can stop CO_2 leaking into the atmosphere

CO_2 saved per year:

3.7 million tons
(● 0.05 tons per person)

Sources: Local government association, 'Growing trees to sequester carbon in the UK: answers to some common questions' by MGR Cannell', Rewilding Britain report / IUCN

Dan Kitwood/Getty Images

How is the UK doing?

Large numbers of new trees are being planted in the UK: this photo shows a man putting in sitka spruces at the biggest forestry scheme in England for three decades, the Doddington North Afforestation Project in Northumberland, launched in 2017. In 2018, the British government gave the go-ahead to plans for the Northern Forest, a woodland stretching from Liverpool to Hull, where 50 million trees will be planted in the next 25 years.

However at the moment the UK is still planting far less than it did 30 years ago: in 1989, 30,170 hectares of new trees were planted, but in 2019 that number will fall to just 13,400 hectares. Almost all of this comes from afforestation in Scotland, which will beat its 10,000-hectare per year target this year: England will plant less than a third of its 5,000-hectare target.

⬥ Climate change activists hold up a banner next to the Bank of England, London, during environmental protests by the Extinction Rebellion group, 25th April 2019

What if the UK took radical action?

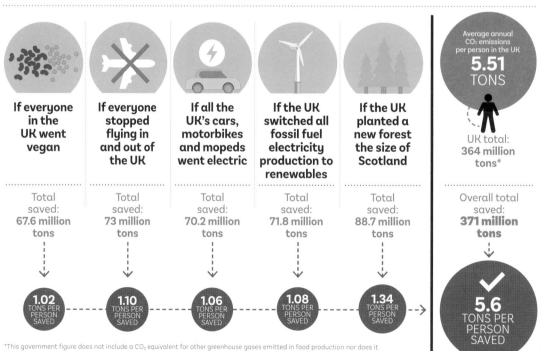

If everyone in the UK went vegan	If everyone stopped flying in and out of the UK	If all the UK's cars, motorbikes and mopeds went electric	If the UK switched all fossil fuel electricity production to renewables	If the UK planted a new forest the size of Scotland	Average annual CO₂ emissions per person in the UK **5.51** TONS
Total saved: **67.6 million tons**	Total saved: **73 million tons**	Total saved: **70.2 million tons**	Total saved: **71.8 million tons**	Total saved: **88.7 million tons**	UK total: **364 million tons*** Overall total saved: **371 million tons**
1.02 TONS PER PERSON SAVED	**1.10** TONS PER PERSON SAVED	**1.06** TONS PER PERSON SAVED	**1.08** TONS PER PERSON SAVED	**1.34** TONS PER PERSON SAVED	✓ **5.6** TONS PER PERSON SAVED

*This government figure does not include a CO₂ equivalent for other greenhouse gases emitted in food production nor does it factor in the European Parliament's increased impact assessment of aviation, as we have in our calculations

Ben Stansall/AFP/Getty Images

SHOP

Missing a back issue, in need of
an infographics print or just fancy
a beautiful Slow News mug?

Head to the DG shop at
slow-journalism.com/DG/shop

Moment that mattered

The UK government moves to revoke Shamima Begum's citizenship

Anthony Loyd, reporter for *The Times* ● INTERVIEW: MATTHEW LEE

"For four years after she left the UK Shamima Begum didn't have her citizenship revoked. Then six days after my interview with her was published [in *The Times* on 13th February], the home secretary Sajid Javid suddenly said he was revoking it. I don't think it's necessary to say too much about Javid's hastiness and opportunism, but it's clear that the decision came after a huge populist swell of rage.

"I wasn't surprised by the intensity of the public interest in my article because when Begum and her two schoolmates ran away from home in east London to join Islamic State in 2015 it was a big story. But I hadn't anticipated the rage. Of course we've had a series of terror attacks in the UK so there is a febrile emotional reaction to anything to do with the Islamic State, but I still believed that since this was about a 15-year-old runaway schoolgirl who had spent the formative years of her life within the caliphate, there would be some kind of concern given the circumstances. I did not anticipate that the nation, by and large, would go batshit crazy.

"I was in Syria on the day of publication. I woke early because I had a long drive out of the country, through quite a bit of Iraq, and to my flight home. I hadn't really looked at the story and by the time I arrived in the UK I was maybe 36 hours behind in realising how big the debate had become. *The Times* encourages journalists to engage with readers in its online comments sections. The people who comment are not necessarily representative of one's readership, and there were some fair, moderate and articulate comments in there, but there were an awful lot more enraged, brutish and hateful comments.

> "This is the first time I've encountered such rage, towards both the subject of the story and the messenger

"This is the first time I've encountered such rage, towards both the subject of the story and the messenger. For the first time in my life I received volumes of hate mail, people calling me a threat to our society and a terrorist sympathiser for suggesting that Begum should be brought home to be investigated. Had this story occurred at a different time in our nation's history, the reaction might have been different. Many of the emotions are less about Begum and more about the confusion and anger in this country at the moment of an identity crisis. The story became centred around who we think we are, who we want in our society and how we deal with people we don't like.

"Some argued that I was giving a platform to an extremist. But the question of what we do with British citizens who joined Islamic State – the fighters, the women, the children – is extremely complicated, challenging and important. I did a very straight-bat interview and the complexity of the case was worked into the story. I didn't feel I was giving a platform to extremist propaganda. I felt I was airing the position of an indoctrinated young woman and British citizen who left the UK as a child.

"I understand the concern that bringing back British jihadists will increase the potential for terror attacks in the UK. But right now we are saying 'don't bring them back, leave them in one of the most insecure places in the world, kettled with thousands of like-minded souls in a country that doesn't want them'. Well, that's not a solution. I'm not sure we've got the legal or prison infrastructure to cope with bringing everyone back, investigating them and putting them on trial. But we can deal with this on a case-by-case basis; first, let's look at the children, who are not guilty of any terror

Former Bethnal Green schoolgirl Shamima Begum, who was discovered in a camp in Syria by Anthony Loyd on 13th February 2019

crime, and work out how to repatriate them. Shamima is a complicated case because she went as a child and became an adult there. I would still say, bring her back and investigate her here.

"Speculating over whether she feels remorse is a ridiculous notion. People were saying 'she wasn't shocked' or 'she wasn't traumatised'. My god, by the time I last saw her, months after our first meeting, she had lost three kids in eight months, been in airstrikes, seen friends of hers killed, been in battles... These commenters have no idea of the extreme stresses of war and child loss. It's ludicrous to think she's not traumatised because she doesn't look traumatised. Yes, she has a slightly odd manner, but I think she'd have that odd manner if she'd stayed in the UK.

"Did I feel sympathy for her? I didn't dislike her. I felt like I was in the presence of a very messed up young woman who made a cataclysmic series of bad choices as a child and has suffered egregiously for those choices. Whether that's sympathy or empathy I'm not sure. In April 2018 I interviewed Alexanda Kotey and El Shafee el Sheikh [British Isis recruits and members of the so-called 'Beatles' terror cell]. Their hostages included friends of mine; some were killed, some survived. It was a complicated interview because I did not like them, but my job was to mask my dislike and learn what I could. They were smart, tough, skilled, highly indoctrinated members of the Islamic State and were totally unapologetic. They had thought through what their position was and how best to play it, and their responses were quite contrived.

"Shamima Begum wasn't like that. She was in a state of shock. She was fresh out the 'caliphate' and it was raw. The way her voice and tone modulated when I asked if she would be a threat to British society... Her brow creased and her face fell and she said 'of course not' - it was very real. She expressed doubt over the 'caliphate' in a camp where she would have been vulnerable to all sorts of intimidation - people had their tents burned down if they spoke out against Islamic State - which suggests to me that her doubts were real. It also suggests the presence of independent thought and that given the correct deradicalisation pressures she could be brought back into the fold. That's not to say that she shouldn't be investigated to see what she did there.

"It's hard to predict what will happen to Begum. I suspect that she will return to the UK at some point as a British citizen for an investigation and trial. I think this will take a long time. Begum is being represented by the lawyer Gareth Peirce, who is challenging the revocation of her citizenship. My understanding is that it's illegal to revoke her citizenship because she is not eligible for Bangladeshi citizenship [as Javid had suggested when explaining his decision] and would be left stateless.

"When I went looking for her I didn't know if she was still alive. I'd been in Baghouz [the last Syrian territory held by Isis, taken by Kurdish-led forces in March 2019] covering the fighting and I became interested in who was leaving Baghouz and where they were going. Women, children and some men, were going to the al-Hawl camp, so I applied for access, went and got turned away. I tried again with the right paperwork, but was told there were no British women there.

"At one point I was chatting with the administration staff in a hut, a conversation going on vaguely over many cups of tea and cigarettes, and a nurse I knew from an NGO walked in. She heard this administrator say that there were no British women in the camp, and when he walked out she muttered to me, 'He's lying'. So I thought 'let's stick with this a bit longer'. It took ages, sitting in this room trying to keep the conversation going, and eventually the administrator said 'OK, look, I'll get you someone'. He said afterwards that he had just walked out and said to a group of women that there's a British journalist who wants to speak to foreign Islamic State wives, and two women stepped forward. One was Shamima Begum.

"Was it a coincidence? It's pretty lucky in a camp of over 40,000 people that the woman I was looking for was within earshot. Maybe there was some serendipity, but I knew where to look. I've spent an awful lot of time in Syria and you begin to get a sense of these things.

"I had a drink with a friend the other day and he told me that the opening line on my Wikipedia entry is 'Anthony Loyd is a British journalist who gained notoriety when he tracked down Shamima Begum'. And I thought 'I've spent 26 years hauling my arse around warzones. I've been in jail several times, been a hostage, been shot, had fucking ten bells knocked out of me in various countries while reporting, and the end result is that I'm notorious on Wikipedia because I found a 19-year-old girl.

"But you know what? I'm really pleased I found her. It's an important story and it's every bit as much about who we are as about who she is." ⑫

> " I felt I was in the presence of a very messed up young woman who made a cataclysmic series of bad choices as a child "

For want of a better word

As 'multipen' ("a pen containing two or more ballpoint refills") is submitted for inclusion in Collins Dictionary, we profile our other favourite suggested neologisms

● RESEARCH: **ROB ORCHARD** ● ILLUSTRATION: **CHRISTIAN TATE**

Featured lexicographers: AustinAllegro, Dipas, Esa50, granddog, karen_tutt, LexicalItem, Muganga0, Mysterick, PooleBeach, ruralgeek

Brexit box (n)
A "Brexit survival kit" containing items such as freeze-dried foods.

Scurryfunge (n)
A hasty tidying of the house between the time you see the neighbour coming and the time they knock on the door.

Yote (v)
Past tense of yeet, to throw with force or lob, e.g. "I yote the bottle at the wall earlier."

Granddog (n)
Canine with similar status to a grandchild.

Idinnerary (n)
The schedule of evening meals for a vacation or business trip.

Chadults (n)
Children who have grown up to be adults.

Dispunctional (adj)
Describes someone who is congenitally incapable of being on time or punctual. Used to describe, for example, someone who always arrives after a meeting has started.

Good aftermorn

16:02

Aftermorn (exc)
A greeting used between people in different time zones wherein one party is still in the morning local time and the other is in the afternoon local time.

Päntsdrunk (adj)
A translation of the Finnish wellness practice *kalsarikänni*, in which one removes trousers and drinks alcohol in the comfort of one's own home.

The age of the ultras

Five years ago groups of violent football fans banded together in the Euromaidan uprising to help depose the Ukrainian president. In the years that followed they have been brought in from the fringes of society and, as **James Montague** reports, are now determined to gain political power in an anxious and unstable country

February 2019

Outside the main municipal building in the Ukrainian capital of Kyiv, just a few minutes walk from Independence Square, Serhii Filimonov and a dozen of his friends and colleagues are unfurling a banner. It's a cold winter morning, grey clumps of snow are piled up on the pavement and the rain is falling harder with each passing minute. Filimonov and his group are here to picket the municipality over a potential real estate agreement that would hand a large chunk of public land to a local oligarch in what they say is a corrupt deal. They plan to reconvene a few hours later at a historical monument in the city to protest the recent killing of a female activist, Kateryna Handziuk.

Handziuk, an advisor to the mayor of Kherson, a city in the south of Ukraine, had become known for exposing local corruption. Her regular Facebook posts didn't discriminate: police officers, government officials and well-known businessmen were all exposed for their alleged wrongdoing. On 31st July 2018, Handziuk was approached by a man who poured a litre of sulphuric acid over her. She received burns covering a third of her body and underwent 11 operations. She died of her injuries five months later. She was 33 years old.

No one has yet been jailed for her killing. "We don't like the events surrounding the investigation into Handziuk," says Filimonov, a well-built man in his mid twenties dressed in the expensive sportswear associated with the 'football casual' subculture. The young men who have joined him are dressed much the same, many with tattoos just about visible as they snake up over their throats or poke out beneath their jacket sleeves. Filimonov's left arm is protected in a brace, his hand bandaged. He says he will keep campaigning until Ukraine's president, Petro Poroshenko, intervenes to ensure that those guilty of Handziuk's murder are brought to justice.

This is how Filimonov fills his days, in a carousel of direct action against what he views as the corrupt elite

○ Serhii Filimonov (second from left), then a leader in the volunteer Azov battalion, stands alongside Andriy Biletsky (left) and other ultra-nationalists after being released on bail from a district court in Kyiv on 10th September 2016

who have operated with impunity for decades and are protected by a captive judiciary. But Filimonov isn't a liberal activist. He is a football ultra, part of a network of organised, hardcore fans known for their colourful choreographies and pyrotechnic displays in the stands. He is the leader of Dynamo Kyiv's most notorious "firm" (an active hooligan faction within an ultras group), the "Rodychi" (The Relatives), notorious for organising fights with other football supporters, often held in forests and fields far from the prying eyes of the police.

Filimonov is also head of the Kyiv division of the National Corps, a political party that is part of an ongoing normalisation of the far right in Ukrainian politics. The National Corps and similar groups are using new tactics that make them hard to pin down, cutting across national barriers and ideological lines as they protest against Petro Poroshenko, their biggest enemy after Vladimir Putin. Poroshenko, an oligarch who made his fortune from chocolate, was elected as the country's first president

> **"**
> This is the head of local police, he is listening to us. We are being watched by spies
> **"**

after the Euromaidan uprising which deposed Viktor Yanukovych. He has overseen a disastrous war in the east whilst the economy has flatlined. His popularity is in the basement and he is lying third in the polls ahead of the presidential elections, due to start in a month.

Such is Ukraine's disillusionment with politics that an actor is leading the polls: Volodymyr Zelensky, a man with zero political experience and an unclear agenda. In the Ukrainian series, *Servant of the People*, Zelensky played Vasyl, a teacher who accidentally became president after a secretly-recorded video of him railing against corruption went viral. For Ukrainians jaded by years of corruption and war, Ukraine's answer to Martin Sheen, who played the US president Jed Bartlet in *The West Wing*, seemed as good a bet as anyone. Filimonov has been busy organising protests at Poroshenko's campaign rallies but today he has more immediate concerns. He nods towards a nearby police officer who is listening to our conversation. "This is the head of local police, he is listening to us," he says. "We are being watched by spies."

⊙ An anti-government protester standing next to burning rubble in Kyiv's Independence Square on 19th February 2014, one of the deadliest days of the Euromaidan revolt

The remains of the day

Today is the fifth anniversary of the bloodiest day of the Euromaidan uprising but Maidan Nezalezhnosti, or Independence Square, is almost empty.

The revolution began in late 2013 when hundreds of thousands of Ukrainians took to the streets to protest against Viktor Yanukovych. The then-president had promised to sign an association agreement with the EU, a signal to the country's young population that Ukraine was seeking a future with closer ties to the west. But Russia opposed the move, as President Putin feared that another key trading partner and strategic asset could be lost to his EU rivals. Yanukovych pulled out of signing the documents under intense pressure from Moscow and major protests erupted across Ukraine in the following weeks, with the biggest taking place in Independence Square.

On 18th February 2014 the stand-off escalated as snipers began killing protesters in Kyiv. Over the next three days, 100 people were killed, the majority on 20th February, the bloodiest day of the revolution. The dead have since been named the "heavenly hundred". A makeshift memorial snakes up one path next to

Independence Square, a long line of temporary shrines each featuring a photo of one of the killed protesters: on the anniversary this year, 100 beams of light were projected into the sky to commemorate them. On 22nd February 2014 Yanukovych fled the capital, headed to his native eastern Ukraine and crossed the border into Russia, where he sought refuge.

The protesters' victory was won with the help of large numbers of organised football supporters – the ultras – who joined with activists in the square. Almost all were from far right ultra groups steeped in a culture of violence and which regularly clashed with one another inside and outside football grounds.

The ultras converged on Maidan and buried their enmity. Former hated rivals joined the same side and, crucially, brought with them the experience of fighting with the police. They gained the respect of even the most liberal protesters for being the muscle of the revolution. They were idolised by far right politicians. "Let us applaud the heroic soccer fans of Dnipro Cherkasy, Kapaty Lviv and Vorskla Poltova!" said Oleh Tyahnybok, the leader of the nationalist, far right Svoboda party at the time. "This is where solidarity starts. This is where patriotism starts."

When Russia annexed Crimea in retaliation for the overthrow of president Yanukovych and fuelled a war in the east by backing pro-Russian separatists, thousands of ordinary Ukrainians volunteered to help their country's woefully underprepared and underfunded military. One battalion of volunteers, Azov, was commanded by a former political prisoner under Yanukovych, Andriy Biletsky. Biletsky had founded the National Socialist Assembly, a coalition of extreme nationalist, radical right and neo-Nazi groups. His aim, according to a 2014 manifesto, was to "lead the white races of the world in a final crusade... against Semite-led Untermenschen." (He has since denied that he ever espoused anti-semitic views).

The bulk of Azov soldiers were drawn from members of Ukraine's ultra groups: Filimonov was one of the first to sign up. They proved to be a fearsome unit and famously retook the strategically vital port city of Mariupol from Russian-backed forces in June 2014. A film, *The Brave Hearts*, was made and shown on primetime TV showing how the ultras had triumphed at Mariupol and made a courageous stand at Donetsk's shattered airport.

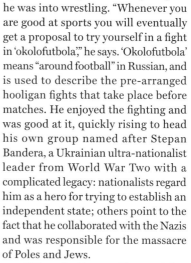

● Azov commander Andriy Biletsky at an oath ceremony for his battalion members in Kyiv on 19th October 2014

In 2016 Andriy Biletsky was chosen to be the leader of Azov's new political wing, the National Corps, and Filimonov was chosen as the head organiser for Kyiv. As quiet as Maidan is on the fifth anniversary of a day freighted with national memories, gazebos have been set up for some of the candidates for the upcoming presidential election. Although it isn't fielding a candidate, the National Corps has its own tent with young men and women handing out leaflets with two pictures on them – of Biletsky and, underneath, of Filimonov.

From hooligan to veteran

Filimonov's office has a brand new reinforced steel door with an electronic security keypad. In the corner is a cabinet designed to house shotguns and ammunition. When I arrive, I find Filimonov sitting behind his large wooden desk examining his injured left arm. "They were beating us so hard," he says. The week before, on Valentine's Day, Filimonov had travelled to Athens to watch his team, Dynamo Kyiv, play Olympiakos in a

Europa League match but had a run-in with Greece's notoriously baton-happy police. "I almost lost my consciousness," he says of the violence he encountered. "I have never been beaten so hard before. My finger could even be amputated."

We are talking in the new HQ of Filimonov's apparently thriving security business, which he runs in between organising and training for football fights and leading the National Corps' Kyiv division. As we talk, dozens of men pass through, all veterans from Azov who have now found employment after their tour of duty finished.

Filimonov explains how he got here. As a young kid he was into wrestling. "Whenever you are good at sports you will eventually get a proposal to try yourself in a fight in 'okolofutbola'," he says. 'Okolofutbola' means "around football" in Russian, and is used to describe the pre-arranged hooligan fights that take place before matches. He enjoyed the fighting and was good at it, quickly rising to head his own group named after Stepan Bandera, a Ukrainian ultra-nationalist leader from World War Two with a complicated legacy: nationalists regard him as a hero for trying to establish an independent state; others point to the fact that he collaborated with the Nazis and was responsible for the massacre of Poles and Jews.

When the Euromaidan uprising began, old football rivalries withered. "Just before to Maidan I was jumped by 20 antifascist fans from Arsenal Kyiv. I was more than angry," Filimonov recalls. Arsenal Kyiv is the only leading club in Ukraine with left-wing ultras. "When Maidan started, I saw the same guys there! But I said this was not the time [for revenge]. So, I shook their hands. We have these ideological and club differences but we shook hands. Maidan was not left-wing or right-wing, Nazi or commie, or whatever. This was the war against Yanukovych."

The days leading up to the bloody denouement of the Maidan uprising were chaotic. The ultras, says Filimonov, took to the front lines "to give people at Maidan a feeling of security and understanding that they are being guarded. They won't fight physically, right? But it gives them the feeling that they have backup and people willing to give up their lives for this noble cause."

❝

Maidan was not left-wing or right-wing, Nazi or commie. It was the war against Yanukovych

❞

GENYA SAVILOV/AFP/Getty Images

○ An instructor for the ultra-nationalist volunteer Azov battalion runs training exercises in Kyiv on 1st March 2015

YURY KIRNICHNY/AFP/Getty Images

As the police attempted to take back the square, Filimonov and about 40 of his fellow ultras ended up being pushed back and cornered. They decided to flee to the Canadian embassy as one of their group had a Canadian passport. After easily pushing past the security, they sheltered there for two days. They even considered applying for asylum in Canada where they could train, regroup and return to fight another day.

The protesters eventually won the day and after Yanukovych fled east, Filimonov left the embassy and began planning for what he believed was the inevitable war to come. He travelled to Dnipropetrovsk in central Ukraine with a group of like-minded Dynamo fans. There he met with ultras from Dnipro, a team that had a friendship with Dynamo. Around 50 of his group volunteered for Azov. Their first taste of action was in Mariupol.

"During the training I only had five bullets. I had a supermarket security uniform," Filimonov says. I ask him about the mission he was assigned. "The storming group," he says. "I was told I must go first into the building and kill everyone." The liberation of Mariupol in June 2014 made Azov's name. After a string of humiliating defeats for the Ukrainian army, it proved that the Russian-backed forces (and Russian troops themselves) could be stopped.

Filimonov's military career would end two months later at post-revolution Ukraine's military nadir: the Battle of Ilovaisk. As many as 1,000 servicemen were killed when a botched raid on the city was followed by a botched retreat, hampered by malfunctioning equipment, poor planning and bad weather. Filimonov was caught in an ambush by pro-Russian forces. "Our commander said we should try to escape but not everyone will survive," he says. "We should run and not stop when someone falls, because it will be our death too." He was badly wounded by a grenade and invalided out of the battalion.

Playing down the right wing

Filimonov doesn't look or sound like a stereotypical fascist. He is young, articulate, charismatic and handsome. He doesn't use overtly racist language. Instead he talks about corruption and bringing oligarchs to justice. His Instagram account is a carefully curated mix of football casual fashion, family-man snaps with his wife and young son and topless shots of him working

⊙ Serhii Filimonov with fellow members of the National Corps in 2016

out or training recruits on how to handle a machine gun. Other photos show him in jail or standing trial, something that happens regularly after he undertakes what he calls "civic action".

As a result of their role in Maidan, and also because of their position as veterans, Filimonov and his ultras have a new, elevated status in Ukraine. Where once they were seen as irrelevant, almost comical characters, they are now feted as revolutionary heroes. "The majority of Ukrainian liberals are in a close relationship with radical nationalists," says Professor Volodymyr Ishchenko, a sociologist at Kyiv's Polytechnic Institute. "They legitimate them, they tolerate and justify their violence. This is one of the biggest problems with civil society."

The National Corps burst onto the scene as a new political force in October 2016 when thousands marched through Kyiv in balaclavas and military fatigues carrying flaming torches. They chanted "Death to enemies!" and "Glory to the nation!" as Andriy Biletsky was voted in as party leader on a four-year term. At the same time a new force, the National Militia, emerged as the militant street wing of the party. "When the authorities are impotent and cannot solve issues of vital importance for society, then simple, ordinary people are forced

to take responsibility upon themselves," Biletsky told Ukrainian media when asked why a political party needed its own militia.

The group is thought to be under the patronage of Ukraine's interior minister Arsen Avakov, who has long ties to the ultra-nationalist movement. It was Avakov's decision to incorporate Azov into the regular army's National Guard. "Although presented as a means to defuse the ultra-nationalist battalion, [this move] led to its explosive growth and branching out into the National Corps political party and increasingly assertive National Militia street movement," wrote journalist Oleksiy Kuzmenko in an investigation for news website *Bellingcat*.

Since Euromaidan there has been a roll call of violent events involving emboldened far-right and openly neo-Nazi groups. According to Kuzmenko's *Bellingcat* investigation, "the National Corps and National Militia threatened a Ukrainian Roma community near Kyiv and later razed the abandoned campsite, streaming the event on Facebook Live." There have since been other attacks on Roma camps, as well as on LGBT events and marches celebrating women's rights. These involved a host of organisations from the same far right eco-systems:

ZUMA Press Inc/Alamy Live News

groups such as C14, Right Sector and Tradition and Order. In all cases the police did little to intervene.

The inaction prompted four prominent human rights groups – Amnesty International, Front Line Defenders, Freedom House and Human Rights Watch – to release a joint, open letter to Avakov. "Hiding under a veneer of patriotism and what they describe as 'traditional values', members of these groups have been vocal about their contempt for and intent to harm women's rights activists, ethnic minorities, lesbian, gay, bisexual, transgender, and intersex people, and others who hold views that differ from their own," they wrote. "The near-total impunity enjoyed by members of groups that promote hatred and discrimination through violent means creates the impression that these attacks are tolerated by the Ukrainian authorities."

The thousand-year city

The National Corps has denied that it is a neo-Nazi organisation. "If the world is worried about the threat of Ukrainian neo-Nazism, I can assure you we are not neo-Nazis; we are simply people who want to change our country for the better," Ihor Vdovin, a spokesman for the National Militia told the *Guardian* in March 2018.

Ukraine's growing far right has often been highlighted in Russia's tightly-controlled media, which frame Euromaidan not as a people's uprising, but an illegitimate fascist takeover abetted by a CIA obsessed with fomenting revolution. As a result, Ukrainian authorities have defensively played down accusations that the far right is gaining a foothold in the country, pointing out that, electorally speaking, all far right groups rarely meet the five percent threshold needed to gain a first MP in parliament. However, the political situation is not as clear-cut as the authorities like to suggest. People do vote for mainstream parties with far right policies, and the second biggest party at the last parliamentary elections was the People's Front, which contains several well known far right figures including Avakov, the interior minister who normalised Azov.

Filimonov denies that he is a neo-Nazi even though some of his associates, identified in the *Bellingcat* investigations, sport Nazi tattoos. To prove that his concern is "corruption, the need to stop stealing" rather than a neo-Nazi agenda, he takes me to a building in

○ National Corps supporters set off flares at an anti-government protest in Kyiv on 2nd March 2019

> ❝
> It was built 1,000 years ago. In Ukraine you had buildings, in Russia only frogs
> ❞

Kyiv that, he says, his group is trying to save from development into a hotel by a corrupt local oligarch he believes is working for Russian interests. On one wall is a huge mural of a snake with Putin's head. He points in the direction of Saint Sophia's Cathedral. "It was built 1,000 years ago," he says. "In Ukraine you had buildings, in Russia only frogs." Ultimately, he believes, fighting corruption will require gaining political office. "For real changes, you need real power," he says.

The next day we meet at Kyiv's Olympic stadium. It is the return match against Olympiakos in the Europa League. The night before, Filimonov's crew went out looking for Olympiakos fans to exact revenge for the events of a week earlier, but to no avail. It is a freezing night but almost 50,000 people are in the stadium. Filimonov arrives late, carrying his young son. "This is his first game!" he says. He's accompanied by Rodion Kudryashov, head of Dnipro's ultras as well as one of the highest ranked members of the National Corps.

Behind us in the upper tier of the stadium a protest begins. Red flares are lit and a banner is unfurled calling for justice for Handziuk, the activist killed by an acid attack in Kherson. The Relatives hooligan faction are relatively small in number, compared to the huge bank of Dynamo ultras on the other side of the stadium. The two sit in separate areas after a falling out between the groups' leaders. So it is important for Filimonov to be there. "I'm here to show my face and shake the hands of the people who have come," he says. Fifteen minutes later he is gone. He misses the celebrations at the final whistle as Dynamo win 1-0.

April 2019

In the build-up to the presidential elections it is widely reported that Biletsky is considering a run, but in the end he does not announce his candidacy.

As the campaigns in Ukraine build to a climax, I watch YouTube videos and news reports of demonstrations. The National Corps and its paramilitary wing, the National Militia, protest in large numbers, often disrupting rallies by President Poroshenko. They are fuelled by a new corruption scandal: allegations that a key presidential ally on Poroshenko's national security council smuggled military parts from Russia and sold them at hugely inflated prices to the Ukrainian army. Thanks to his arm brace I can spot Filimonov at the front of the protests, trying to herd and organise hundreds of men dressed all in black. The disruption of rallies becomes so bad that ambassadors for the G7 issue a public letter to interior minister Avakov calling for him to intervene in the campaign to guarantee free and fair elections.

In an extraordinary case of life imitating art, on 21st April the comedian and political novice Volodomyr Zelensky is elected president in the second round of voting, winning 73 percent of the poll to Poroshenko's 25 percent. "I will never let you down," he tells a group of cheering supporters. "Everything is possible."

"I'm usually pessimistic because the state is very weak in Ukraine and it will get weaker," says Professor Ishchenko of the country's prospects under its new leader. "Economic prospects are poor. There are deep cleavages exploited by political parties. This is all looking pretty bad. There is some hope in Zelensky. But whatever good intentions he has there are very strong structural problems [that are] unlikely to be solved in the near future. Ukraine's future is more likely to be decided in Moscow, Brussels and Washington than Kyiv."

In one of his first acts, Zelensky moves the elections for the Ukrainian parliament forward from October to July, likely too soon for the National Corps to make a breakthrough. Party leader Biletsky agrees a pact with the far right Svoboda and Right Sector parties in the hope of reaching the five percent threshold and gaining an electoral upset. When the combined 20 person list is announced, Filimonov is not on it.

○ Comedian Volodymyr Zelensky gives a victory speech in Kyiv after winning the second round of the election on 21st April 2019

> ❝
> The far right can't win a seat in parliament but they have militias, veterans, arms, training... They dominate the street
> ❞

He quits the party in the days after the announcement, citing a corruption scandal at Azov, and says he will form his own political group, tentatively called 'Honour'.

The far right faces challenges breaking out of its role on the street and into parliament, says Professor Ishchenko, but that is not the only way to wield power in Ukraine. "They cannot win elections but so what?" he says.

"Elections are an important indicator. But only one. It's like in France, the Rassemblement National [formerly the Front National] scores 20 per cent. That is a big problem. But on the other hand, how many battalions do they have? Zero. Here the major far right groups can't win a seat in the parliament, but they have militias, veterans, arms, training. Electorally they are weak, but in extra-parliamentary terms they are among the strongest groups in civil society. The far right dominate the street. They have the strongest street movement in Europe."

Filimonov continues to push his activist agenda. Next on the list is a street campaign to grant citizenship to the foreign fighters from Russia, Belarus, Croatia and beyond who joined Ukraine's volunteer battalions. In some cases, they have effectively been rendered stateless. "It is vital for them to get Ukrainian citizenship," he says. "They can't go home, because they'll be imprisoned there." There are also some football fights arranged with other firms across Europe to train for, once his finger has fully healed. A procession of confrontations beckons – against fellow ultras, oligarchs, politicians and the separatists in the east.

He has a surprising confession to make, for an ultra. "I don't like football," he admits. "But I like it when we win a tough game." ⬮

NOTES

On the blog: A compilation of DG stories on Ukraine can now be found on our website at slow-journalism.com/blog

From issue #14:
An interview with one of the investigative journalists who gained access to the lavish abandoned mansion of **ousted leader Viktor Yanukovych** and sifted through troves of financial documents.

From issue #26:
We visited Crimea over a three-year period to assess **the impact of the Russian annexation** and Western sanctions on its population.

From issue #31:
We dived into the incredible story of **Arkady Babchenko**, the Russian journalist whose killing was faked by the Ukrainian authorities to foil a Russian assassination plot.

The movie matrix

February's film releases in order of critical reception and box office success

● WORDS AND RESEARCH: MARCUS WEBB

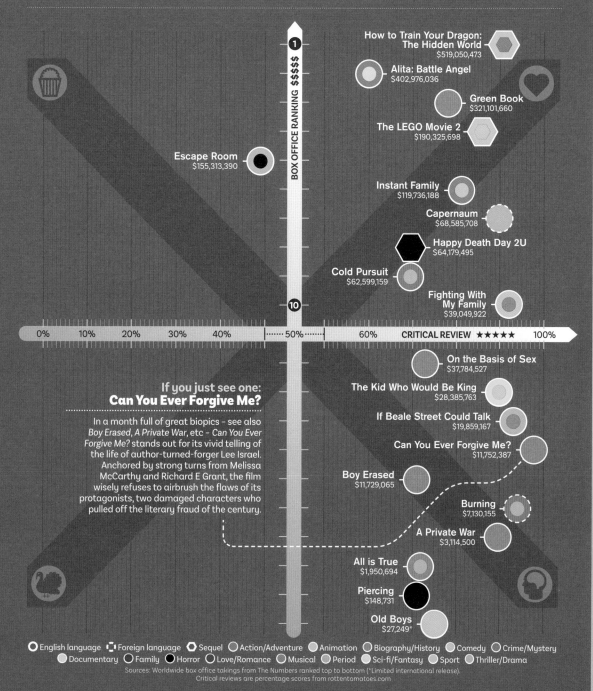

BOX OFFICE RANKING $$$$$

1

10

How to Train Your Dragon: The Hidden World
$519,050,473

Alita: Battle Angel
$402,976,036

Green Book
$321,101,660

The LEGO Movie 2
$190,325,698

Escape Room
$155,313,390

Instant Family
$119,736,188

Capernaum
$68,585,708

Happy Death Day 2U
$64,179,495

Cold Pursuit
$62,599,159

Fighting With My Family
$39,049,922

On the Basis of Sex
$37,784,527

The Kid Who Would Be King
$28,385,763

If Beale Street Could Talk
$19,859,167

Can You Ever Forgive Me?
$11,752,387

Boy Erased
$11,729,065

Burning
$7,130,155

A Private War
$3,114,500

All is True
$1,950,694

Piercing
$148,731

Old Boys
$27,249*

0% 10% 20% 30% 40% 50% 60% **CRITICAL REVIEW ★★★★★** 100%

If you just see one:
Can You Ever Forgive Me?

In a month full of great biopics - see also *Boy Erased, A Private War,* etc – *Can You Ever Forgive Me?* stands out for its vivid telling of the life of author-turned-forger Lee Israel. Anchored by strong turns from Melissa McCarthy and Richard E Grant, the film wisely refuses to airbrush the flaws of its protagonists, two damaged characters who pulled off the literary fraud of the century.

● English language ◌ Foreign language ◇ Sequel ○ Action/Adventure ○ Animation ○ Biography/History ○ Comedy ○ Crime/Mystery
○ Documentary ○ Family ● Horror ○ Love/Romance ○ Musical ○ Period ○ Sci-fi/Fantasy ○ Sport ○ Thriller/Drama

Sources: Worldwide box office takings from The Numbers ranked top to bottom (*Limited international release).
Critical reviews are percentage scores from rottentomatoes.com

MAR

Almanac

The month's news in brief ▼

● EDITED BY: MATTHEW LEE

The story behind the shot

Contestant Jazell Barbie Royale of the US is crowned Miss International Queen 2019 at the transgender beauty pageant in Pattaya, Thailand on 8th March. Royale is the first black woman to take the crown since the event started in 2004. Her win means that for the first time in history Miss USA, Miss America, Miss Teen USA and Miss International Queen are all women of colour.

Jewel Samad/AFP/Getty Images

Fri 1st

NETHERLANDS ◉ The Organisation for the Prohibition of Chemical Weapons (OPCW) confirms that chemical weapons were used in an attack on the Syrian town of Douma in April 2018 which killed more than 40 people. The Hague-based watchdog says its data show that a toxic chemical containing reactive chlorine was used in the attack on the rebel-held town, which the UK, US and France blamed on Syrian government forces.

Sat 2nd

US ◉ Bernie Sanders launches his campaign to be president in 2020. At an event in his native Brooklyn, the 77-year-old 'democratic socialist', who lost to Hillary Clinton in the Democratic primaries for the 2016 election, vows to build the "strongest grassroots coalition in the history of American politics".

Sun 3rd

US ◉ A test flight by SpaceX's Dragon capsule successfully docks with the International Space Station. It is one of several tests Elon Musk's rocket company needs to pass before its crew capsule, which carried only a test dummy and 180kg of supplies on the 27-hour journey to the ISS, can gain approval from Nasa to transport astronauts.

Mon 4th

DENMARK ◉ A major study involving 650,000 Danish children confirms that there is no link between autism and the vaccine which protects against measles, mumps and rubella. Although 1998 research linking autism to the MMR jab by gastroenterologist Andrew Wakefield has been discredited, a global 'anti-vax' movement has been growing. On 26th March, Rockland County in New York declares a state of emergency following a severe outbreak of measles, which authorities blame on anti-vaxxers.

Tue 5th

UK ◉ New research published in *Nature* claims that a second person has been cured of HIV following cancer treatment. An anonymous 'London patient' was freed of the virus after receiving transplanted bone marrow from a donor with a rare genetic mutation of the CCR5 gene, which is associated with HIV resistance. The findings arrive more than a decade after Timothy Brown, aka the 'Berlin Patient', became the first person to be cured of the virus.

SPAIN ◉ Champions League holders Real Madrid are eliminated from the competition in a shock 4-1 home defeat to Ajax. The Amsterdam club had lost the home leg of the tie 2-1.

Craic addicts

A new report by the US National Retail Federation claims St Patrick's Day is the third 'booziest' day in the US, behind Mardi Gras and New Year's Eve, but how Irish were this year's revellers?

9.6%

 Percentage of US population with Irish ancestry

55%

Percentage of US population that planned to celebrate St Patrick's Day in 2019

Sources: US Census Bureau, US National Retail Federation

 (Wed 6th)

UK ◎ Geoffrey Cox arrives home empty-handed from Brussels talks over the Irish 'backstop'. The UK attorney general had hoped to receive "reasonable assurances" from EU lead negotiator Michel Barnier that the arrangements for the Irish border would not become permanent.

(Thu 7th)

UK ◎ The Queen posts on Instagram for the first time. The monarch, who has already tweeted and posted on Facebook, uploads a letter sent by computing pioneer Charles Babbage in 1843 to her great-great-grandfather Prince Albert to the Royal Family's Instagram account.

US ◎ A Virginia court sentences Paul Manafort to 47 months in prison for a variety of bank and tax fraud charges. Five days later the former Trump presidential campaign chief is sentenced to a further three-and-a-half years at a separate trial in Washington DC for felonies including money laundering,

unregistered lobbying and obstruction of justice.

(Fri 8th)

US ◎ Chelsea Manning is jailed for refusing to testify before a Virginia criminal inquiry into WikiLeaks. The 31-year-old, who leaked thousands of US military documents to Julian Assange's anti-secrecy website in 2010 and whose 35-year prison sentence was commuted by Barack Obama in 2017, objects to the secrecy of the grand jury process.

(Sat 9th)

JAPAN ◎ A 116-year-old woman is confirmed as the world's oldest living person in a Guinness World Records ceremony in Fukuoka City. Kane Tanaka was born in January 1903.

Record breakers

233.24m
Longest kneeling golf shot
Wed 13th
Shinobu Saeki, Hira Golf Club in Otsu, Shiga, Japan

8.458m²
Size of largest magazine ever published
Thu 14th
Pressgraph in Barcelona, Spain

574
Most people eating breakfast in bed
Sat 30th
Cappy, Johannesburg, South Africa

 (Sun 10th)

ETHIOPIA ◎ All 157 people on board Ethiopian Airlines Flight ET302 are killed when it crashes shortly after take-off.

(Mon 11th)

IRAN ◎ A prominent human rights lawyer is sentenced to a total of 38 years and 148 lashes in a secret trial, according to her husband. Nasrin Sotoudeh, who has

---

represented women arrested for removing their headscarves, was charged with insulting Iran's supreme leader, spying and spreading misinformation about the state. Reza Khandan says that due to Iranian law his wife will only serve 12 years of the sentence in prison.

MALAYSIA ◎ An Indonesian woman accused of killing the estranged brother of North Korean leader Kim Jong-un is released from prison after a Malaysian court drops the case against her. Siti Aisyah, who along with Doan Thi Huong was accused of killing Kim Jong-nam by wiping a toxic nerve agent on him in Kuala Lumpur airport in February 2017, claimed she had been told by North Korean agents that the material was harmless and she was participating in a prank for a Japanese TV game show. On 3rd May, Huong flies home to Vietnam after pleading guilty to a lesser charge.

 (Tue 12th)

UK ◎ Theresa May's Brexit deal is defeated by MPs for a second time. May loses by a margin of 149 votes and says she "profoundly regrets" parliament's decision.

US ◎ The justice department accuses over 50 people including business leaders and celebrities of participation in a nationwide college admissions scam. It is alleged that parents paid a well-connected middleman to help them use fraudulent techniques, such as cheating in tests and bribing sports coaches, to get their children into elite universities. William Singer, the architect of the scheme, pleads guilty to four charges in a court in Boston, Massachusetts.

 (Wed 13th)

US ◎ Boeing grounds its entire global fleet of 737 Max planes. Its decision,

Kyodo News

🏛 Pale, male and frail

In March, *Forbes* released its annual list of the world's billionaires. The 20 wealthiest people on the planet have assets of $1.2 trillion between them. But who owns what?

WEALTH OWNED BY THE PLANET'S TOP 20 BILLIONAIRES...

$ 1,207,200,000,000

Who are **OLD** (over 70)

$ 637,500,000,000

Who are **WHITE**

$ 1,118,400,000,000

Who are **AMERICAN** (US citizens)

$ 917,000,000,000

Who are **MEN**

$ 1,187,500,000,000

Who are **OLD, WHITE, AMERICAN MEN**

$ 544,000,000,000

Of which
$82,500,000,000
is owned by
Warren Buffett

---

which comes after the aircraft was grounded by almost all of the world's aviation authorities, was triggered by the identification of similarities between the Lion Air plane crash in October 2018 and the Ethiopian Airlines crash on Sunday 10th March.

📖▶ P090
'Moment that mattered'

US ○ The boss of the notorious Gambino crime family is shot dead outside his home in New York City. Frank Cali is the first mob boss to be killed in the city since 1985. In late March a murder suspect, 24-year-old Anthony Comello, appears in court with the Trump campaign slogan 'MAGA' and a large letter Q written on the palm of his hand, assumed to

refer to the baseless 'QAnon' online conspiracy theory, which argues that Donald Trump is working to expose a global liberal paedophile ring

EL SALVADOR ○ The country's supreme court temporarily halts the cancellation of a free trade agreement with Taiwan amid speculation that the country's new leader may reverse his predecessor's decision to recognise China over the disputed country and switch allegiances back to Taipei.

📖▶ P094
'The isolation of Taiwan'

 Thu 14th

IRELAND ○ A new report claims the global lithium ion battery market will

grow by eight times in the next six years, from $7 billion at the end of 2018 to $58.8 billion by 2024.

📖▶ P096
'Battery farming'

 Fri 15th

NEW ZEALAND ○ Fifty-one people are killed and 50 more are wounded in shootings at two Christchurch mosques.

📖▶ P104
'Moment that mattered'

MOZAMBIQUE ○ Cyclone Idai makes landfall in the centre of the country, devastating the coastal city of Beira.

📖▶ P108
'Through hell and high water'

 Sat 16th

UK ○ Wales beat Ireland 25-7 to win the Grand Slam in the Six Nations rugby tournament.

 Sun 17th

US ○ Northern Irish golfer Rory McIlroy wins the Players Championship title at Ponte Vedra, Florida.

 Mon 18th

NETHERLANDS ○ A gunman kills four people on a tram in Utrecht. Four days later 37-year-old Gokmen Tanis confesses to the shooting and says that he acted alone.

PHILIPPINES ○ It's reported that a whale that washed ashore on the island of Mindanao had 40kg of plastic bags in its stomach.

🥚 Famous for five minutes

Will Connolly, aka 'Egg Boy'

Will Connolly was so incensed by the remarks of Australian senator Fraser Anning after the shootings in Christchurch that he took matters – and an egg – into his own hands. Anning had blamed the killing of 51 people in two mosques by a far-right gunman on 15th March on New Zealand's immigration policy, and a day later Connolly splatted the politician with an egg during a TV interview. In the ensuing scuffle the 17-year-old was twice punched by Anning. Footage of the incident went viral and funds for Connolly's "legal fees" and possibly "more eggs" were raised by supporters online. The police chose not to press charges, meaning that in May Connolly could donate the AU$99,922 (£55,000) raised to Christchurch Foundation and Victims Support.

 Tue 19th

KAZAKHSTAN ◗ Nursultan Nazarbayev resigns as president after three decades in charge. The 78-year-old, who has been in power since independence and whose regime has faced accusations of human rights abuses, will remain head of the governing party. The following day Kassym-Jomart Tokayev is sworn in as president and the capital, Astana, is renamed Nursultan in honour of Nazarbayev.

 Wed 20th

UK ◗ MPs criticise the BBC for going over budget in building a new set for its soap opera, *EastEnders*. The public accounts committee is concerned that licence-fee payers are not getting value for money from the E20 upgrade project, which is running five years behind schedule and is now on track to cost £87m – £23m more than anticipated.

Thu 21st

BELGIUM ◗ EU leaders agree to offer the UK a two week extension to find a solution to its Brexit crisis.

UK ◗ The Tate galleries say they will no longer accept donations from the

---

Born

Stadia
New cloud-based game-streaming platform from Google, designed to bring an end to console boxes and enable the company to dominate the gaming industry. Announced **Tue 19th**

Arifa Sultana's surprise twins
Children born to Bangladeshi mother Arifa Sultana 26 days after she gave birth to her first child. Doctors attending Sultana, 20, had not realised she had a second uterus, a rare congenital condition, or that she was carrying two additional children. Born **Thu 21st**

New White Hart Lane
The state-of-the-art, £1 billion Tottenham Hotspur stadium reopens with a capacity of 62,062. Reopened **Sun 24th**

Died

Luke Perry
Actor on TV series *Beverly Hills, 90210* and *Riverdale*, 52. **Mon 4th**

Keith Flint
Lead singer with The Prodigy, 49. **Mon 4th**

Wow Air
Seven-year-old Icelandic airline, goes into administration after failed attempt to sell to IcelandAir, **Thu 28th**

Sacklers, the US family whose pharmaceutical company, Purdue Pharma, has come under scrutiny for its alleged role in creating the opioid addiction crisis in the US through its marketing of prescription painkiller OxyContin.

 Fri 22nd

US ◗ Special counsel Robert Mueller's inquiry into Russian interference in the 2016 election is delivered to the attorney general, William Barr. Two days later Barr publicly releases a four-page summary of the report, which states that no evidence of collusion between the Trump campaign and Russia was found. On 18th April a redacted version of the document is made public.

Sat 23rd

UK ◗ Hundreds of thousands of people march in London to demand a second Brexit referendum.

SYRIA ◗ The Syrian Democratic Forces declare a final victory over Isis after winning a battle for the village of Baghouz, the last piece of the Islamist group's territory in the country.

 Sun 24th

NORWAY ◗ A cruise ship docks safely after an engine failure in bad weather required a major evacuation effort, which saw nearly 500 of the 1,373 people on board airlifted to safety. After regaining power, the *Viking Sky* was accompanied by tugboats as it completed its journey to the port of Molde.

NIKLAS HALLE'N/AFP/Getty Images | YouTube

Victory : Defeat

Tue 12th An unnamed punter at the Cheltenham Festival wins £182,567 from a £2 bet after picking a placed horse in each of six races.

Wed 13th A 43-year-old Australian man in Nimbin, New South Wales, is confronted by an assailant wielding a bow and arrow and starts recording the encounter on his iPhone. He narrowly avoids serious injury when the arrow pierces his iPhone rather than his head.

Sun 24th Food bloggers Kate Allinson and Kay Featherstone see their slimming cookbook, *Pinch of Nom*, sell 210,506 copies within three days, making it the fastest-selling non-fiction book in the UK since records began in 2001.

Thu 7th Detroit rapper Jonathan Woods, aka Selfmade Kash, famed for rapping about his skill at credit card fraud, is charged with credit card fraud by federal prosecutors.

Wed 20th Catherine Blaiklock, co-founder of the month-old Brexit Party, resigns after she is challenged by *Guardian* journalists about anti-Islamic messages she posted on Twitter before starting the party.

Mon 25th A British Airways flight from London City Airport to Düsseldorf in Germany lands in Edinburgh by mistake, with passengers only discovering the change when a "welcome to Edinburgh" announcement is made. Incorrect flight paperwork is blamed.

Fleabag vs Best in Show

(A) **Mon 4th** The second series of acclaimed sitcom *Fleabag* debuts on BBC1 (B) **Sun 10th** Planet Waves Forever Young Daydream Believers, aka Dylan the Villain, becomes the first papillon to be named Best in Show at the Crufts dog show

Source: Google Trends, based on Google searches in March. Lines represent the popularity of each search term relative to the other on each day of the month.

OLI SCARFF/AFP/Getty Images

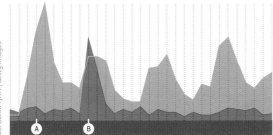

 Mon 25th

MONTENEGRO A European Championship qualifying match is overshadowed by local fans' racist abuse towards black English players. Montenegro coach Ljubisa Tumbakovic says he "didn't hear" the racist abuse during England's 5-1 victory in Podgorica. On 26th April, Montenegro is ordered by Uefa to play its home game against Kosovo behind closed doors as punishment.

 Tue 26th

UK The government rejects an online petition to revoke Article 50 and remain in the EU, stating that it cannot "break the promises" to leave the EU made to voters. The petition, which goes on to be signed by more than six million people, was started by 77-year-old Margaret Georgiadou.

 Wed 27th

INDIA Prime Minister Narendra Modi announces that India has destroyed its own low-orbit satellite with a ground-to-space missile, heralding the country's breakthrough as a military space power. Five days later Nasa head Jim Bridenstine describes India's anti-satellite weapons test as a "terrible thing", claiming that the 400 or so pieces of debris it created now pose a threat to astronauts on the International Space Station.

 Thu 28th

UK A woman who can barely feel pain helps doctors identify a new genetic mutation that could potentially help in the treatment of people with chronic pain, according to new research published in the *British Journal of Anaesthesia*. 71-year-old Jo Cameron, who says that when she accidentally burns herself she knows about it

from the smell of burning flesh rather than any pain, is one of only two people in the world known to have the genetic mutation, known as FAAH-OUT, that suppresses pain and anxiety.

UK Ole Gunnar Solskjær is appointed the permanent manager of Manchester United.

 Fri 29th

UK Theresa May loses a third meaningful vote on her Brexit deal on the day the UK was originally scheduled to leave the European Union. The defeat by a margin of 58 votes takes place as thousands of Leave supporters protest the delay outside parliament. On 11th April the EU agrees to extend Article 50 to 31st October.

 Sat 30th

VENEZUELA Nicolás Maduro makes a deal with the Red Cross to deliver humanitarian aid inside the country. The embattled president had previously denied that there was a humanitarian crisis in Venezuela.

 Sun 31st

TURKEY The ruling AK party loses control of capital Ankara and Istanbul to candidates from the main opposition Republican People's Party in local elections. President Recep Tayyip Erdoğan's party complains about alleged irregularities in Istanbul and in May the result is cancelled by the authorities and a rerun scheduled for June.

Moment that mattered

Boeing's entire global fleet of 737 MAX aircraft is grounded after a second crash

Sally Gethin, aviation analyst ● INTERVIEW: MATTHEW LEE

On 13th March Boeing announced that it would ground all 371 of its 737 MAX planes in operation around the world due to safety concerns. The US plane-maker's CEO Dennis Muilenburg said his company "continues to have full confidence in the safety of the 737 MAX" and that the move is a "proactive step out of an abundance of caution". Aviation authorities around the world had already banned the plane from their airspace following the crash of Ethiopian Airlines Flight 302 three days earlier, which saw all 157 people onboard killed when the plane crashed six minutes after take-off. It was the second disaster involving the Boeing aircraft in less than five months, following the Lion Air crash of October 2018 in Indonesia which killed 189 people.

"I was very cautious in the early stages after the Ethiopian crash," says Sally Gethin, an independent analyst who runs the Gethin's Inflight News website. "But people were quickly making the assumption that there were similarities to Lion Air." Analysts were able to get in-depth information on flight-tracking website Flightradar24, which in both cases showed a new Boeing 737 MAX 8 plane plunging minutes after take-off.

The preliminary evidence from both crashes suggested that the pilots struggled against Boeing's automated flight software, known as the Maneuvering Characteristics Augmentation System (MCAS), which automatically lowers the aircraft's nose using stabilisers on the tail to prevent it from stalling and crashing. "It seems so innocuous, this one little electronic device," says Gethin. "How could this one little gizmo bring down an aircraft?"

"It seems so innocuous... How could this one little gizmo bring down an entire aircraft?"

An update of Boeing's long-standing 737 workhorse, the MAX is a single-aisle plane with improved fuel efficiency, which the company hoped would help it compete with rival Airbus and its fuel-efficient A320neo model. "The problem with the MAX is its aerodynamics – the centre of gravity is different [to the older 737]," Gethin says. "They took the skinny airframe of the 737 and plunked massive great engines in it, which sit further forward. This means that when aircraft get airborne they tend to create a lot of speed and thrust and force the nose up. Boeing created MCAS to counteract the changed aerodynamics and make the plane safe, but the pilots were in a new situation. In both these tragedies the pilots were flying what seemed to them a very familiar aircraft, the old 737, but this was a quite different plane."

According to preliminary evidence from air crash investigators in Indonesia and Ethiopia, the angle-of-attack (AOA) sensors on both planes sent incorrect data to MCAS indicating that the nose was pointing too high. MCAS responded by pushing the nose down to what it believed was a safe angle, but was in reality dangerously downward-facing. On the Lion Air flight it has been suggested that the pilots, who were unaware of the presence of MCAS, were able to temporarily counteract the software, but that the AOA sensors continued to send false data, resulting in a tug-of-war the pilots didn't win. After the Indonesian crash Boeing issued new safety recommendations, yet the Ethiopian authorities say its initial investigations suggest that the pilots followed these recommendations and still failed to get the plane under control.

A tiny piece of technology has come to play an outsized role in the analyses of the crashes. "These

◑ Grounded Boeing 737 MAX aircraft at Southern California Logistics Airport, 27th March 2019

aircraft didn't have what's called a 'disagree light,'" says Gethin. "This light would have shown the pilots that the AOA sensors were giving false readings, but it turned out that disagree lights were optional features." The light was not available as standard and around 80 percent of Boeing customers, including Lion Air and Ethiopian Airlines, didn't pay for the separate cockpit indicator that was required for it to function. However, it is unclear whether a functioning disagree light would have saved any lives. Boeing says that the feature wasn't necessary for safe flying.

The US regulatory body, the Federal Aviation Administration (FAA), initially affirmed its faith in the plane after the 10th March crash, even as aviation authorities around the world issued bans. But on 13th March it buckled and grounded the 737 MAX. Three months later the planes remain grounded and there is no indication of when they will fly again. Boeing initially said it expected to fix its software in weeks, but weeks became months and as of mid-June both Boeing and the FAA said there was no timeframe for getting the MAX airborne again.

"One estimate is that for every month the MAX is grounded the cost to the industry is $1.5 billion," says Gethin, explaining that there is tremendous pressure on Boeing to fix the problem from airlines which staked their future on MAX orders, and which now have numerous $100 million aircraft sitting in hangars. Southwest Airlines, the biggest customer of the aircraft in the US, is cancelling around 130 flights a day. Although Boeing's cash reserves have been depleted by at least $1 billion due to the grounding, mainly because of a halt in jet deliveries, this is unlikely to be an existential crisis for the company, which last year saw record revenue of $101 billion.

The reputational hit to Boeing caused by the two incidents, however, was considerable. This was compounded by a series of reports in the *New York Times* in the weeks after the second crash which claimed that Boeing rushed through the 737 MAX project to maintain a competitive advantage with Airbus and that after the Indonesian crash American Airlines pilots, who were frustrated that nobody had told them about MCAS, were rebuffed by Boeing officials when they asked for the apparent flaw to be urgently dealt with.

Boeing also admitted that it discovered back in 2017 that the disagree light wasn't functioning unless airlines had paid for optional equipment, and that it had withheld the information until after the Lion Air crash, when it informed the FAA.

The FAA's role in the crisis has also come under scrutiny. "What's coming out of this whole apocalyptic story is that there was too cosy a relationship between Boeing and the FAA," says Gethin. "They designated Boeing staff as their regulators. Clearly there's a massive conflict of interest." On 11th April the *New York Times* reported that the FAA didn't conduct any safety reviews of critical changes to MCAS, which made the system active in a broader range of situations.

It remains to be seen whether travellers will want to fly in the 737 MAX in the future. "We're seeing a backlash amongst the travelling public," says Gethin. A June survey showed that only 14 percent of passengers would definitely fly on the 737 MAX within six months of it being returned to service. More than 40 percent would book more expensive or less convenient flights to avoid the aircraft. "The $64 million question is whether people will get back on board the 737 MAX in the kind of numbers to make it cost effective for the airlines to still operate it," Gethin says. "The memory of the travelling public is notoriously short, but there isn't any sign of public nervousness abating at the moment and don't forget we're going to have lots of lawsuits keeping the story in the news cycle."

These lawsuits are from shareholders, over the alleged concealing of safety deficiencies, airline pilots and the families of the bereaved.

Three months of reporting on a major corporate crisis has perhaps overshadowed the human tragedy – 346 passengers were killed in the two crashes. "We still don't yet have the full and final report of the Ethiopian Airlines crash, and the Lion Air incident is still an ongoing investigation," says Gethin, adding that we have no idea how long it will take. For the victims' families, the wait for definitive answers might be a lengthy one.

Boeing received an unexpected shot in the arm at the Paris Air Show on 18th June when IEG, the multinational that owns British Airways, bought 200 737 MAX aircraft in an order worth more than $24 billion. "It might look like it's all come to a screaming halt but these aircraft are still being rolled off the assembly line in anticipation of going back in to service," says Gethin. "In many ways it's business as usual for Boeing."

> "
> One estimate is that for every month the MAX is grounded the cost to the industry is $1.5 billion
> "

Delayed Gratification

THE SLOW JOURNALISM MAGAZINE
ISSUE 30

- Salisbury's toxic shock ● How to clone a white rhino ● The inside story of March for our Lives
- The billionaires' race to space ● A return to Homs ● The 17th century roots of the KFC crisis
- Plots and pucks in Pyeongchang ● What do Britons want? ● All the slow news that mattered

THE SLOW JOURNALISM COMPANY
LAST TO BREAKING NEWS

SAVE

Subscribe now to save **25% off the single issue price***, receive your issue before everyone else and **support the Slow Journalism revolution.**

*Cost of buying four individual issues online = £48

slow-journalism.com/subscribe

THE PERFECT GIFT

Two million

Estimated number of refugees who flee to Taiwan with nationalist leader Chiang Kai Shek in October 1949 following defeat by the Communists under Mao Tse-Tung in the Chinese Civil War. Mao declares the creation of the People's Republic of China (PRC), while Chiang Kai Shek establishes Taipei as the new seat of his government.

81

Miles between China and Taiwan at the narrowest part of the Taiwan Strait. On 27th June 1950, in reaction to the North Korean invasion of South Korea, President Truman deploys the US Seventh Fleet to patrol the strait, leading Mao Tse-Tung to abort a plan to invade Taiwan, and creating a de facto commitment to US protection of the island.

58,000

Troops sent by Chiang Kai Shek to the Kinmen islands in August 1954, where they create new defensive structures. The islands sit 1.2 miles east of the mainland Chinese city of Xiamen: the Chinese react by shelling the islands, leading to two 'Taiwan Strait crises' in the 1950s in which the two sides fight over Kinmen and other neighbouring islands.

37

Countries that switch their diplomatic recognition from Taiwan to China between 1949 and the end of the 1960s, including the Soviet Union in 1949, the UK in 1950 and France in 1964.

54

Percentage of the vote won by Lee Teng-hui in a landslide victory in Taiwan's first democratic presidential elections in 1996, a year after rejecting offers of bilateral talks from Chinese President Jiang Zemin.

Two

Chinese fighter jets that cross the median line in the Taiwan Strait for the first time in almost 20 years in March 2018, leading Taiwan to scramble aircraft to intercept them. A month later the US approves the sale of submarine technology to Taiwan.

100

Percentage of the 44 airlines presented by China with a demand to list Taiwan on their websites as being part of China that capitulate by a deadline of 25th July 2018, under threat of unspecified punishment. The last to give in are American Airlines, Delta and United Airlines.

17

Countries that still formally diplomatically recognise Taiwan, after El Salvador cuts ties on 20th August 2018. This dwindling band (average population: 3.12 million, average GDP: $9.55 billion) does not have the clout to bring pressure to bear on the PRC.

Wed 13th MAR 2019

The isolation of Taiwan

The quarter was marked by escalating tensions between China and Taiwan – as the atmosphere becomes increasingly bellicose we take a look at the numbers behind the 70-year journey that brought us to this point

● RESEARCH: ROB ORCHARD ● ILLUSTRATIONS: CHRISTIAN TATE

Sources: ABC, BBC, CNN, Defense News, Reuters

76

Countries that support a successful resolution sponsored by Albania at the UN in October 1971 recognising the People's Republic of China as "the only legitimate representative of China to the United Nations." The resolution ejects Taiwan from the UN and gives its seat on the permanent security council to the PRC.

29

Years after Chiang Kai Shek's flight to Taiwan the US establishes official relations with the PRC. In January 1979 the US replaces its diplomatic relations with Taiwan with a 'Taiwan Relations Act' under which it can still supply arms to the island. Beijing issues a 'Message to compatriots in Taiwan', claiming a desire for peaceful reunification.

Three

Noes in the new policy declared in April 1979 by President Chiang Ching-kuo of Taiwan in reaction to the 'Message to compatriots in Taiwan': no contact, compromise or negotiation with China.

33,000

Height in feet at which pilot Wang Shi-chuen attacks his fellow crew members with an axe, hijacks their China Airlines cargo plane and flies it to Guangzhou on 3rd May 1986. Taiwan is forced to negotiate with Chinese officials in Hong Kong over the return of the crew, thereby establishing de facto contact between the two sides.

330 million

Value in US dollars of arms sales approved by the US to Taiwan in September 2018. The Chinese army (2,035,000 personnel) is seven times larger than its Taiwanese counterpart (290,000). China's economy is 19 times larger, its population is 58 times larger and its landmass is 265 times larger than Taiwan's. In December 2018 the US passes the Asia Reassurance Initiative Act, reaffirming its commitment to Taiwan.

40

Years to the day after the 'Message to compatriots' when Chinese president Xi Jinping calls for the "reunification" of China and Taiwan, suggesting he will be prepared to use force against "separatist activities" and describing foreign interference in the issue as "intolerable". In reaction to Xi's 2nd January 2019 statement, Taiwan's military deploys combat helicopters and tanks to beaches on its west coast in a show of force.

Two

Number of US Navy warships that sail through the Taiwan Strait on 24th January 2019. Another sail-through follows in April, the fifth since the US resumed the practice in July 2018 in defence of its "freedom of navigation".

54

Percentage of the vote in the El Salvadorean presidential election won by political outsider Nayib Bukele on 3rd February 2019. In a small potential piece of good news for Taiwan, Bukele, who takes office in June 2019, has questioned whether El Salvador should maintain diplomatic relations with China or return to recognising Taiwan. On 13th March 2019 El Salvador's supreme court halted the cancellation of a free trade agreement with Taiwan.

Just Seventeen

The territories that continue to formally recognise Taiwan:
Belize, Eswatini, Guatemala, Haiti, Holy See, Honduras, Kiribati, Nauru, Nicaragua, Paraguay, Palau, the Marshall Islands, Solomon Islands, St Kitts and Nevis, St Lucia, St Vincent and the Grenadines, Tuvalu

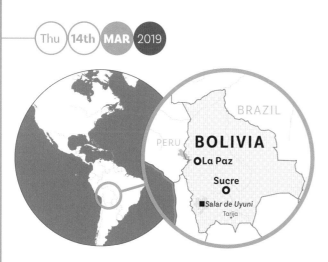

BRAZIL

PERU

BOLIVIA

○ La Paz

Sucre
○

■ Salar de Uyuni
Tarija

Battery farming

A worldwide boom in green transport has created an increased demand for lithium, one of the key metals used in the production of batteries for electric vehicles. Photographer Matjaz Krivic, who has been documenting the lithium industry for three years, traces its path from the salt flats of Bolivia to the battery factories of China and on to the roads of Europe and the US

● WORDS: MARCUS WEBB ● PHOTOGRAPHY: MATJAZ KRIVIC

"I've been following the lithium chain since the start of the modern lithium rush in 2016. There were lots of lithium mines in the world in the '80s, particularly in the US where lithium was stockpiled for use in nuclear weapons, but they were mostly closed down as the stockpiles were sold off after the cold war and the price of lithium fell. However, the move towards electric cars and the desire to clean up the air in our cities has seen lithium come back in a big way.

"The early electric cars used lead batteries, but lithium batteries are lighter and charge faster so for powering vehicles they are better in nearly every way; there's nothing else that comes close at the moment. But the electric car industry needs a lot of lithium – a large smartphone has about two grams of lithium in it, while there's an estimated 63 kilograms in an electric car. This new demand saw the price of lithium double between 2016 and 2018. Suddenly Bolivia, which has over half of the known remaining reserves of lithium – an estimated 16 million tonnes – found itself at the centre of this new world."

All images: Matjaz Krivic/INSTITUTE

Salt miners at work in Bolivia's Salar de Uyuni. Locals have found themselves competing for water with the lithium plants in a desert where there is little to no rain between April and September

"There are a number of different ways of getting lithium out of the ground, and the process they use in Bolivia isn't really mining at all. Most of the lithium is contained in a mineral-rich brine around ten metres beneath Salar de Uyuni, the world's biggest salt flat, in the remote south of the country. Workers drill though the crust until they hit a reserve that is high in lithium, which they then pump into shallow reservoirs where it is left for months at a time for the water to evaporate. This leaves behind a brown sludge containing a mixture of manganese, potassium, borax and lithium salts, which is then filtered and placed into another evaporation pool, and the process begins again. It can take up to 18 months before the mixture has been distilled enough to extract the lithium carbonate.

"The process destroys the pristine condition of the salt flats, one of Bolivia's great national treasures. But the biggest impact of lithium exploitation in Bolivia has been on the local communities, which have traditionally depended on local quinoa farming and salt mining. Lithium processing uses a lot of water - approximately 500,000 gallons per tonne produced - and to supply it the government has started diverting water away from neighbouring villages and towns into the new lithium plants. All mining has an environmental impact, even if it ultimately leads to green technology."

○ Vehicle tracks run across the salt flats of Salar de Uyuni
○ Miguel Parra, head of production at Comibol's Llipi lithium plant, shovels "white gold"

"President Evo Morales of Bolivia said that Bolivia, Latin America's poorest nation, could become 'the Saudi Arabia of lithium', with the mineral mining bringing in a new era of wealth like oil did to the Middle Eastern country. But this won't be straightforward.

"The process used in Bolivia takes time, and can't be scaled up quickly in response to new demand.

Faster processes are being developed and new mines opened in other countries, including Chile, which is currently producing 100 times as much lithium as Bolivia. Morales has been anxious not to allow international companies to come in and dominate the industry, with all lithium exploration, prospecting and mine development in the country run solely by state-owned mining company Comibol. This changed recently when Bolivia signed exploitation contracts with German and Chinese companies which should see production increase considerably.

"Unlike oil, lithium can be reused and recycled. Less than two percent of lithium batteries are currently recycled, but if this changes we could see the price of lithium go down as a result. However, even while the prices are high, I didn't see many people in the local area around Salar de Uyuni benefiting from the resources below the surface. The process does not require a lot of labour so the new plants aren't generating a lot of employment. The lithium has been extracted for years and I haven't seen anything significant coming back to the local community."

◉ A worker looks out over the Llipi lithium plant
◉ Lithium evaporation pools in the middle of the salt flats of Salar de Uyuni

○ The production line at lithium ion battery company Soundon New Energy's factory on the outskirts of Xiangtan, China
○ Tesla Model 3 cars in Norway, February 2019. During March 2019, 58 percent of all new cars sold in the country were fully electric

"While Bolivia has the raw materials, China totally dominates the world of lithium batteries. If you want to get batteries you pretty much have to go through a Chinese company. Even Panasonic, the Japanese company that provides batteries for Tesla, outsources to China.

"I visited the main factory of Soundon New Energy, one of China's largest battery manufacturers, on the outskirts of the polluted city of Xiangtan in Hunan province. I expected it to be a sweatshop, full of manual workers, but it wasn't like that at all – it was like looking into the future. Everything is automated, there are robots moving around with cameras and sensors directing them so they don't bump into each other. I think the four people I photographed [see left] assembling parts were the only people in the entire factory who weren't working behind a computer.

"Europe and America are way behind when it comes to this technology. China needs to take action or it will choke to death on pollution and the government is forcing environmental measures through. To register a non-electric car in Beijing you need to enter a lottery. If you don't get it you will have to go without a vehicle for a year before you can try again, so people will have to make the move to electric.

"There are around 200 companies in China that only produce electric vehicles – in the West there is only one really established company: Tesla. And it's not just cars - China is making electric trucks, electric buses, electric mopeds, electric tractors, everything. To fuel it they need more and more lithium and they are tying up sources all over the world: Bolivia, Chile, countries across Africa – even the US. I spoke to somebody in the States who was prospecting for lithium. I asked him who he would sell it to if he found it and he was certain it would be a Chinese company, because they paid the most. This was 300 kilometres from the Tesla factory.

"At the moment there is plenty of lithium to go around. But when electric cars really take off across the world, which could be in a couple of years, then there will be a bottleneck and I think there's the potential for conflict and trade wars.

"Despite the disruption I have seen lithium mining cause, I am not an electric car sceptic. If you can power cars with renewable energy, then they have to be better for the environment than burning oil. To produce an electric car you have to use a lot more metals such as copper and lithium than a traditional combustion engine, but once it is on the road it is much more efficient, there's less to break down and those materials can be reused or recycled afterwards. It is the future - but I don't think anyone predicted we would get there so quickly." ◉

NOTES

The end of the ICE age?

While no country has yet committed to an outright ban on traditional internal combustion engines (ICE), some have set targets and timelines for phase-outs of diesel and petrol vehicles...

By 2020	**Austria** No new ICE vehicles sold (excluding hybrids)
By 2021	**Costa Rica** Initiate complete phase-out of ICE vehicles
By 2025	**Norway** No new ICE vehicles sold
By 2030	**Denmark** No new ICE vehicles sold (excluding hybrids) **Germany** No registration of ICE vehicles **India** No new ICE vehicles sold **Ireland** No new ICE vehicles sold **Israel** No new ICE vehicles imported **Netherlands** No new ICE vehicles sold
By 2032	**Scotland** No new ICE vehicles sold
By 2035	**Denmark** No new ICE vehicles sold (including hybrids) **Taiwan** No new ICE motorcycles sold
By 2040	**UK** No new ICE vehicles sold **China** No new ICE vehicles sold **France** No new ICE vehicles sold **Taiwan** No new ICE vehicles sold

Moment that mattered

Fifty-one people are killed in mass shootings in Christchurch

Yan St-Pierre, security consultant ● WORDS: MATTHEW LEE

On the afternoon of 15th March, a far right extremist opened fire on worshippers at the Al Noor mosque in Christchurch, New Zealand. He then drove to the Linwood Islamic Centre and opened fire again. The attacks, in which 51 people were killed and dozens more wounded, were the country's deadliest mass shootings, described by prime minister Jacinda Ardern as one of New Zealand's "darkest days". The victims, the youngest of whom was three years old, came from all over the world, many of the families having moved to New Zealand to escape violence and persecution.

The gunman, 28-year-old Australian Brenton Tarrant, initially faced multiple murder charges. But on 21st May, having consulted with survivors and the families of victims, police added the charge of terrorism. For Berlin-based counterterrorism advisor Yan St-Pierre, the additional charge is a key detail. "The argument against bringing terror charges is that a murder charge already comes with one of the harshest penalties, so it almost feels redundant and it complicates a case," says St-Pierre. "Yet charging the gunman with terrorism helps tackle the cultural bias associated with far-right terrorists as compared to Islamist terrorists. I spoke to many people in Quebec about Alexandre Bissonnette [a white Canadian who killed six people and injured 19 others at a Quebec City mosque in January 2017] and the response tended to be 'He had psychological issues – is it really terrorism?' There's a reluctance to acknowledge that far right extremism can be a product of our communities. But when far right violence is treated as terrorism it's made clearer that society is part of the problem."

St-Pierre says that charging a single perpetrator such as Tarrant with terrorism is complicated because in most Western countries counterterrorism laws are designed for people who are part of a network. Yet he believes that there is some kind of broader structure at work behind many attacks characterised as 'lone-wolf', such as Christchurch. "Even if attackers appeared to be operating alone, there's nearly always a broader network at play," he says, adding that charging somebody with an act of terror increases the chances of identifying and dismantling these networks. "People know of Isis and Al-Qaeda, but the public is unaware of the equivalent groups on the far right. But these groups exist and they will claim an attack like Christchurch is carried out in their name."

In May it was revealed that Tarrant had given money to Martin Sellner, the leader of the 'Identitarian movement' in Austria. Followers of the movement, which has branches in many Western countries, promulgate 'replacement theory', the racist notion that immigration and multiculturalism is intended to make white people a minority "in their own countries". Before the attack began, Tarrant had emailed a sprawling "manifesto" supposedly detailing his motives to media outlets – he titled it 'The Great Replacement'. Tarrant had connections with proponents of this racist doctrine around the world, and his Facebook followers were the first to know about his attack – he live-streamed it on his page. Although Facebook quickly removed the footage it was shared widely on other platforms. St-Pierre believes that the video will have a malign impact for many years. "The medium really was the message in this case and people watched it, commented on it and shared it. It was a horribly effective use of a modern communication method."

> " People know of Isis and Al-Qaeda, but the public is unaware of the equivalent groups on the far right "

Hagen Hopkins/Getty Image

Prime Minister Jacinda Ardern hugs a worshipper at Kilbirnie Mosque in Wellington two days after the worst mass shooting in New Zealand's history

○ Police surround Al Noor mosque in Christchurch following the attack on 15th March

St-Pierre says that technology has brought about what he calls "the democratisation of extremism". "Extreme opinions used to be shared in closed circles but now there's the capacity to spread propaganda widely and see it filter into the mainstream," he says.

Two months after the attack, world leaders and representatives from big tech firms met in Paris to sign the 'Christchurch call', an agreement organised by Jacinda Ardern and French president Emmanuel Macron. Describing the initiative as a "roadmap to eliminate terrorism from the networks", Ardern hopes that tech companies and signatory nations will work together to develop and utilise technology to keep extremist violence off the internet. In a further response to the attack, Facebook changed its livestream rules to exclude those who break its hate speech guidelines.

Tarrant's decision to livestream his attack was widely interpreted as demonstrating the gunman's craving for notoriety. In an address to parliament in Wellington on 19th March, Jacinda Ardern said that she refused to give him what he wanted and would never use his name. "If every attacker for every terrorist incident is not named it will have a positive impact," says St-Pierre. "But if we don't name a far-right attacker but then name someone affiliated to Isis it could be dangerous. People in Muslim countries are saying that names such as Mohammed have been associated to terrorism for years so why shouldn't Brenton be the same? I think either you don't say the name of any terrorist or you say the name of them all."

Two days after her address to parliament, Ardern announced an overhaul of New Zealand's gun laws. Assault rifles and military-style semi-automatics would be banned and a buyback scheme would be introduced. "Gun laws can have an impact," says St-Pierre, "but if someone wants to commit a terrorist act they will find a weapon, maybe a car or a knife, so changing gun laws can feel like focusing on the symptoms rather than the cause." St-Pierre believes that a more proactive approach is required. "We need to get ahead of the game and that starts with recognising incidents like Christchurch as acts of terror and tackling the networks and messages that enable them. Otherwise the terrorists will always be in front."

The counterterrorism challenge is becoming tougher than ever, says St-Pierre. "Terror has become even more multifaceted," he says. "Right now we are mostly dealing with religious terrorism, left and right-wing extremists and violent environmental activists. But there is an ever-greater pool of people willing to act violently upon their political ideas and grievances: that's the biggest challenge we face." ®

Fiona Goodall/Getty Images

Celebrity tree count

As the *MailOnline* reports that Angelina Jolie wore a black camisole and matching leggings to a meeting, we calculate how many trees were felled to bring us the rest of March's celebrity gossip

● RESEARCH: MARCUS WEBB

How it works:
We measured the amount of paper used for each story and multiplied it by the latest audited circulation of the publication and the GSM (grammes per square metre) of the paper to discover the overall weight. Environmental impact estimates were then made using the Environmental Paper Network Paper Calculator Version 3.2 (for more information visit c.environmentalpaper.org), factoring in the specific paper type of each publication. All estimates are approximate and rounded to the nearest tree.

Sarah Hyland wore two pairs of Spanx at the same time ⓗ

Nicole Appleton enjoyed a mini break ⓞ

Rochelle Humes looks like her sisters ⓗ

Josh Denzel always sees **Liam Payne** at the gym but is too shy to say hello ⓒ

Anna Kendrick bought some toilet paper in a supermarket ⓗ

James Arthur went to Center Parcs ⓗ

Mark Wright's mum might look after the baby he is thinking of having ⓗ

Binky Felstead is looking forward to Mothering Sunday ⓗ

Amy Childs thinks there's more to life than vajazzles ⓒ

Robbie Williams wants everyone in America to know who he is ⓗ

It rained when the **Duke and Duchess of Cambridge** visited Blackpool ⓗ

Publications: ⓒ Closer · ⓗ Heat · ⓗ Hello! · ⓞ OK!

Taking covers

Celebrities whose image appeared on the most front covers of the big four gossip mags this month

The Duchess of Sussex
11 covers

Victoria Beckham
Nine covers

The Duchess of Cambridge
Eight covers

Katie Price
Seven covers

Billie Faiers
Six covers

Through hell and high water

On 15th March Cyclone Idai made landfall at Beira in the central region of Mozambique, leaving devastation in its wake. Just six weeks later Cyclone Kenneth crashed in over the city of Pemba in the north, inflicting widespread destruction. In the aftermath of the storms **Harriet Salem** travelled across Mozambique to meet some of the victims and to uncover the web of circumstance and corruption that make this beautiful country so vulnerable to natural disasters

Elisa Jorge clung to the tree for dear life. All around her she could hear babies crying and parents calling for their children. In the darkness she thought she could feel snakes and insects crawling over her skin, but to let go of the branches and swat them away would have meant falling to her death in the raging waters below. She sang hymns to herself to try to keep awake.

It felt like an eternity but when daybreak finally came, some neighbours stranded on a nearby roof were able to throw Jorge a rope and pull her to relative safety. They could see bodies floating past in the swirling river that had submerged their small village near Búzi in Mozambique, in one of the regions worst affected by Cyclone Idai. "It was like hell there. We had no food or clean water. We had nothing except the clothes we were wearing and our prayers," Jorge tells me.

Eventually after four long, hungry days, those prayers were answered as rescuers in speedboats arrived to take them to safety. As they made their way down the river, they saw countless others still trapped by the floods, who shouted for help as they passed. But there was no more room in the boat. "We didn't stop," says Jorge, wiping a tear from her cheek with the back of her hand.

Cyclone Idai had made landfall near Beira, Mozambique's second-largest city, halfway up its coastline, on 15th March. The sea surged by four metres and the storm deposited torrential rains, causing rivers to burst their banks in its wake. At least 1,000 people were killed by devastating winds and by floods which stretched over more than 1,200 square miles. Thousands more people are still missing and aid agencies say the true death toll may never be known. Branded among "the worst weather-related disasters" ever to have affected

A resident of Búzi, Mozambique, stands amid the ruins of his home, destroyed by Cyclone Idai, 22nd March

An aerial photo shows a flooded area of Buzi in central Mozambique, 20th March

Picture: Getty Images

the southern hemisphere by the World Meteorological Organisation, Idai was followed just over a month later by Cyclone Kenneth, the strongest storm to hit Mozambique since modern records began.

Still affected by the legacy of Portuguese colonial rule and the fallout from a bloody civil war that only ended in 1992, Mozambique is already among the poorest nations in the world. Now it faces a new challenge: life at the sharp end of climate change.

Many fear that Idai and Kenneth are signs of what is to come. To date, only nine storms of a tropical cyclone intensity have ever been recorded making landfall in Mozambique. For two to hit the country in such quick succession is "extremely worrying" says Acacio Tembe, director of the weather prediction department at Mozambique's Institute of Meteorology, who has worked monitoring storms over the Indian Ocean for more than 20 years. He is also worried by the timing and location of the cyclones. Both hit outside Mozambique's usual 'season' – which runs from the beginning of January to the end of February – and none has ever hit as far north as Kenneth did. "It's not possible to say if it's part of a trend or a one-off yet," says Tembe. "We will have to wait and see – but it's not a good sign."

Someone else's bar fight

The Institute of Meteorology in which Tembe works is housed in a grand-looking colonial building in Maputo, the capital of Mozambique. Its walls are painted a dashing canary yellow and its garden is well maintained, but a glance at the top floor reveals crumbling brickwork and broken windows. In one of its offices, spokesman Bernardino Nhantumbo sits next to a creaking, whirring fan, a bead of sweat glistening on his forehead. It's more than 30 degrees outside and stiflingly hot even in the shaded interior of the building.

Despite having one of the lowest carbon emissions in Africa, which has the smallest carbon footprint of all the continents, Mozambique's geographical position places it on the front line of the effects of global warming. Or, as Nhantumbo jests darkly, "It's like when someone else picks a fight in a bar, but when you turn around, they've run away and they've left you standing there alone!"

◔ Acacio Tembe, director of the weather prediction department at Mozambique's Institute of Meteorology

> ❝
> It's not possible to say if it's part of a trend or a one-off yet. We will have to wait and see – but it's not a good sign
> ❞

Nhantumbo mops his brow with a pocket handkerchief as he clicks through files on his computer, hunting for a slide-show presentation on climate change he delivered the week before. The institute has manifold problems, he informs me as his computer hums worryingly loudly. One is the issue of its outdated equipment which, much like the exterior of the building, is long overdue some investment. Then there are the low wages and a lack of qualified staff. On the shelf behind him sits a stack of books. At the top of the pile is a well-thumbed copy of *An Introduction to Dynamic Meteorology*. "It's very hard to keep the skilled people in Mozambique. Those that have a good education leave to work for international organisations that pay better money," he explains.

The Notre Dame Global Adaptation Initiative ranks Mozambique 13th in its list of the countries most vulnerable to climate change-induced extreme weather. According to a USAID report, between 1961 and 2010 average temperatures in Mozambique rose by around two degrees. Meanwhile the number of "hot days", on which temperatures reach above 35 degrees, has doubled in the last three decades. By 2050, climate change researchers predict temperatures could go up by another 2.5 degrees in some regions of the country, with even the most optimistic models still forecasting a one-degree additional rise.

Just one degree of additional warming would have a devastating impact on Mozambique's economy and food supply. More than a quarter of the country's gross domestic product is accounted for by agriculture and up to 70 percent of the population are subsistence farmers, depending on their own crops to survive. Small changes in weather, says Nhantumbo, can destroy a harvest and "make the difference between feast and famine".

Severe storms in this region are not unusual, but the scientific consensus is that their intensity and severity will increase as temperatures across the globe keep going up. Cyclones need several concurrent ocean and atmospheric conditions to form. Among them is a sea surface temperature of 26.5°C or above, with high-intensity storms only forming at 28°C or higher. Parts of the Indian Ocean now reach up to 32°C. Meanwhile, rising air temperatures mean more moisture in the atmosphere, bringing heavier rains when storms come.

Adrien Barbier /AFP/Getty Images | Harriet Salem

On top of that, the sea level along Mozambique's 1,550 miles of shoreline has risen by 3cm since 1961 and is predicted to rise by up to 56cm by 2090 as glaciers continue to melt around the world. With an estimated 60 percent of Mozambique's population – around nine million people – living in low-lying coastal and river delta areas, flooding and rising sea levels threaten to displace many in the coming decades if global warming continues apace. "If something doesn't change, we'll all end up underwater," says Nhantumbo bluntly.

Pointing to a map on his computer screen, Nhabtumbo's colleague Tembe traces the looping route that he watched Idai wind through the Mozambique Channel. A sliver of the Indian Ocean, measuring around 260 miles at its narrowest point and around 1,000 miles in length, it separates Mozambique from Madagascar. The neighbouring island has, until now, acted as a natural storm shield for much of the Mozambican side of the channel, taking the brunt of incoming cyclones, which then usually dissipate and weaken.

This was not the case with Cyclone Idai, however, which barrelled around the country's coast before making landfall not once but twice. The torrential downpours it brought caused both the Pungwe and Búzi rivers to burst their banks, sweeping entire communities away in their wake and creating what Mozambique's president, Filipe Nyusi, called an "inland ocean" reaching several hundred miles into the interior of the country.

The damage was aggravated by Mozambique's poor infrastructure. Although North America frequently experiences cyclones as intense as Idai and Kenneth, its buildings are designed to withstand extreme weather events. Mozambique's are not.

Many homes in the country, particularly outside cities and in poor neighbourhoods, are built from cheap local materials – usually a mud-concrete mix that quickly disintegrates when submerged in water. Roofs are often little more than corrugated steel sheets or palm tree branches strapped together. Even the sturdier concrete buildings are often poorly maintained. "It's this combination that made it so bad," says Tembe. "We had rain followed by high winds then more heavy rain. In these conditions, the buildings just fall down."

⊙ A woman walks past destroyed houses in Mozambique's Cabo Delgado province, 13th May 2019

> " We had rain followed by high winds then more heavy rain. In these conditions, the buildings just fall down "

"A rich country, with poor people"

Eric Charas is a stocky, energetic Mozambican who speaks excellent English with an American lilt. He's enthusiastic and outraged in equal measure, characteristics that help make him a good activist.

We meet at 'Casa Jovem' – Houses for Youth – on the outskirts of Maputo. It's Charas's latest 'social justice project' and he's keen to take me on a tour. The apartment complex is an unremarkable maze of breezeblock flats, serviced by a shop and a small café. What makes it unique, however, are the below-market prices aimed at allowing young first-time buyers to get on the property ladder with just a small deposit, with the outstanding balance paid off through rent. "This project is the first scheme of its kind," says Charas with pride. "We hope it's a first step in reducing Maputo's high youth homelessness rate."

The state-run press has branded the housing complex a failure, citing slow progress and building regulation issues, but Charas waves away the criticism. "Sure, it's a failure," he says with a chuckle. "Look around you, houses are being built and bought; people are living here. We're doing it and they're not. They don't like that at all – the fact they're saying this means it's a success, otherwise they'd say nothing. That's how Mozambique works."

By 'they' Charas means the government, of whom he's a vocal critic. As well as managing Casa Jovem, he's the publisher of an independent newspaper. *Verdade* (*The Truth*), which claims to have a circulation of around 600,000, making it among the most-read media outlets in the country. Journalism is a high-risk profession in Mozambique and Charas's activities have got him in trouble more than once. He estimates he's been to court nearly 30 times. "It's an annoyance" he says, but so far at least he's been "lucky to just be harassed and not locked up".

On the day I meet Charas, *Verdade* has a big scoop on its front page. The environment minister has been caught on tape in a phone call discussing a host of illegal activities, including bribe taking, with the former administrator to the president's office. Charas is not surprised. The newspaper editor can reel off a long list of "scandals" if, he says sardonically, "you can even still call them 'scandals' when they're so routine".

○ People wait for a delivery from the World Food Programme in the wake of Cyclone Idai. After losing a harvest and livestock in the flooding, many in Mozambique are dependent on international organisations

Among them is the 2018 discovery of some 30,000 'ghost' workers in the public sector receiving a combined pay cheque of nearly £200 million over two years and, in 2013, the revelation that nearly half of Mozambique's vast timber exports to China – up to 48 percent, or around 215,000 cubic metres of timber, that year – were illegal. The latter scandal allegedly involved the former minister of agriculture as well as numerous other officials charged with protecting the country's forests. "Destroying the environment to line his own pocket. Well what does that tell you about the state of things?" asks Charas.

But perhaps the most flagrant instance of corruption, and certainly the costliest to the country, was the so-called 'secret loans' scam. In 2016, Kroll, a New York based risk-management company, revealed that the government led by former president Armando Guebuza had taken out $2 billion (£1.57 billion) in undisclosed state-backed loans three years earlier. The money, borrowed from Russian bank VTB and Swiss bank Credit Suisse, was ostensibly to set up a state-run tuna-fishing company, but was later found also to have been used to buy overpriced maritime security equipment, including military-grade speedboats that are still sitting unused in Maputo's docks.

In practice much of the rest of the money, at least £393 million, disappeared. The exposure of the theft was ruinous for the country. The International Monetary Fund suspended its funding to Mozambique's government, a catastrophe in a country that receives about a quarter of its budget from foreign donors. Economic growth shrank by nearly half in a year – from 6.6 percent in 2015 to 3.8 percent in 2016 – and the currency nosedived, devaluing by 65 percent in just six months.

"Imagine if even a tiny fraction of that money had gone towards projects to build schools and hospitals, or roads, or to teach people about the environment," says Charas. "It's staggering, mind-blowing, when you look at the poverty in this country and think about all the things it could have been used for."

"I'm ranting," he says, pausing to catch his breath. "But the point is, Mozambique is not a poor country, it's a rich country with poor people." It's a persuasive argument. In 2009, the world's largest deposit of rubies was discovered in the blood-red soils of Montepuez, a province in the north-east of the country, by a local farmer. Today, Mozambican rubies account for around 80 percent of global output and the gems, which are prized for their clarity, fetch prices of up to £549 per carat. As

○ Pastor Itamar Fernandes stands by his car, destroyed by his church's roof, which was torn off when Idai hit Beira

well as rubies, Mozambique sits on substantial reserves of gold, platinum, diamonds, iron ore and aluminium. There are also 25.6 billion tonnes of unexploited coal, its largest export.

The most lucrative of all the country's resources, however, is set to be natural gas. In 2011, oil and gas giants Eni from Italy and Anadarko from the US discovered a 150-trillion-cubic-foot gas field off Mozambique's northern coast; it is the world's fourth-largest offshore reserve, worth hundreds of billions of dollars. The discovery has been heralded as a potential turning point that could transform Mozambique from a developing nation into a solid middle-income country.

To date, however, little of Mozambique's vast natural resource wealth has trickled down to the people. Only around a quarter of the country's population have access to electricity and less than half have clean drinking water. Although the number of people living in extreme poverty has fallen slightly in recent years, 48 percent of Mozambicans still live on less than $2 (£1.57) per day. In rural regions that figure rises to 80 percent. This subsistence lifestyle leaves ordinary Mozambicans completely unable to adapt to or mitigate the worst excesses of their changing climate.

The church without a roof

Pastor Itamar Fernandes built the Missao Africa Pieia Evangelical Church in Beira himself. When I meet the Brazilian missionary his jeans and T-shirt are covered in dust and his hands are dirty. He's spent the morning picking up the pieces of his life's work.

On the night Idai hit Beira, Fernandes took his wife and three young children and hid in an outhouse, figuring that it was the strongest shelter on the grounds. Crouched on the floor they prayed as the winds roared around the building. Juju, a pet monkey belonging to the church, screamed and rattled the bars of his cage in panic as the cyclone ripped the church's roof clean off and sent it crashing down onto the pastor's car. The building's windows were smashed and the walls of the Bible-study classrooms and toilets collapsed. "We lost everything that we worked for 22 years to build. Now we have to start again from scratch," Fernandes tells me.

It's a Sunday and volunteers from the church are perched on ladders, stringing up tarpaulin over what was once the roof in a bid to protect the congregation from the blazing heat of the sun. A mural of a Mozambican landscape on the church's far wall blends seamlessly

Harriet Salem

into the bright blue sky. The damage hasn't deterred worshippers from attending mass, though, and by midday the room is packed. The service is loud and upbeat. A gospel choir leads hymns, children read poems and the pastor, now changed into a smart suit, booms his sermon through a microphone. The crowd respond with plenty of rapturous hallelujahs.

At the end, Fernandes says some prayers for the victims of Idai and Kenneth before inviting the congregation to come forward and make donations towards the church's repairs. Most do, but he says it's unlikely to cover even a fraction of the costs. "They give what they can, but they are poor people so even sparing a few coins is a big act of charity," he tells me.

After the service, Fernandes takes me to visit the Grande Hotel Beira. Built in Art Deco style, with an Olympic-sized swimming pool and sea views, this establishment was one of Africa's most luxurious resorts in the 1950s and '60s. Today it houses the poorest of the poor. There's no electricity or running water. The swimming pool, filled with a murky green-brown sludge, is used by residents to bathe and wash their clothes. Most of the building's floors have been ripped up to use as fuel for cooking fires.

An estimated 1,500 squatters live here, among them 350 orphans supported by Fernandes's church. He gestures to the nearby ruins of a building, which used to house the children in their own separate quarters before Idai tore it down. Now the kids are living in some of the hotel's former guestrooms. It's noisy, cramped and basic, the walls are streaked with dirt and the mattresses, lying side-by-side on the floor, are thin and threadbare.

"For now, it's the best we can do. It's not ideal – this is a dangerous place," says Fernandes. "There are drug addicts and criminals living here. We're hoping to raise some more money and rebuild the orphanage, but that's going to take time." Before we leave he says some prayers with the children, who sit in neat rows on the floor waiting for volunteers to hand out their daily food ration. It's meagre: the younger children, aged four or under, get two bread rolls, and those who are older get only one. "It's always those that already have the least that suffer the most in these situations," Fernandes says with a sigh as we leave.

Across the city I hear similar tales of woe. Mohammed Zobura lives in an 'accommodation centre' for people displaced by the cyclone near Beira's port,

a prime piece of real estate. Little more than some ramshackle rows of dusty tents, currently housing several hundred families, the camp is a jarring contrast when compared to its immediate neighbour, the Marina Casino. A gambling mega-complex for wealthy Mozambicans and Chinese businessmen, it has a luxurious swimming pool, giant dragons flanking the doors and a car park filled with four-by-fours and limousines.

Along with his wife and four children, Zobura shares a small tent with five other families. At night they sleep on a tarpaulin ground mat, squashed in side by side. The Zobura family have been living here for the past three weeks since their home washed away in the floods that followed Cyclone Idai. Like many staying here, they are from Praia Nova. The neighbourhood, which nestles against Beira's beachfront, is home to many of the city's fishermen and some of its poorest residents. Most of the houses in the district were built from cheap materials that were unable to withstand the winds and rains.

> " Only around a quarter of the country's population have access to electricity and less than half have clean drinking water "

"First, the roof collapsed and then the waters started to come in, up to here," Zobura says, gesturing to his waist. "Very fast and from every direction. Our road turned into a river." He and his wife scooped up their children, grabbed what they could carry and headed for higher ground. As they waded away, they looked back and saw their possessions and furniture floating away on a torrent of water towards the sea. "That's all we managed to take," he says pointing to a few pots and pans and a small suitcase in the corner containing some clothes.

Like the Zobura family, most of those still living in the camp – around 1,200 people – simply have nowhere else to go. Although the camp is meant to be a temporary measure, it's already showing signs of becoming at least semi-permanent. Some of those living here have set up little 'shops' outside their tents selling soap and other basic goods and an NGO-funded school is being run under sheets strung up on wooden poles.

Rebuilding and getting families like the Zoburas out of their tent cities will be a big and costly task. An estimated 230,000 homes were either damaged or destroyed by Idai across central Mozambique. An initial post-disaster risk assessment conducted by the United Nations has estimated that around £2.5 billion is needed to restore infrastructure and social services in the areas affected by both Kenneth and Idai. However, two international donation drives have only raised around half that amount so far.

The destroyed harvest

I travel from Beira to the inland town of Búzi in a minibus, the most common form of public transport in Mozambique. Known locally as a *chapa cem*, it's seen better days: the suspension is shot and the broken sliding door has to be tied shut with a rope, creating a terrible rattling whenever the vehicle moves. The conductor squeezes in as many passengers as possible: 18 adults, two children, one baby and a furiously squawking chicken.

The road we take as we head out of the city doesn't exist on Google Maps, and only partially exists in real life. As we cross the Pungwe River a thick fog descends. The reeds on the riverbank are only just visible through the mist and the temperature drops sharply, prompting my fellow passengers to scrabble around under the seats and in their bags for jumpers and woolly hats. After around 40 miles or so, we pass a road digger and a group of workers with drills. Shortly afterwards the asphalt abruptly ends. The rest of the way is a dirt track and the driver doesn't slow down for potholes. It takes four-and-a-half long and bumpy hours to reach our destination.

Although Mozambique's road network has improved in recent years, due in large part to substantial investment by China, it is still among the worst-connected countries in sub-Saharan Africa. Only 20 percent of the country's roads, around 3,700 miles, are paved with asphalt, and most of those run east to west, connecting major urban hubs to ports, but not to each other. The setup, or rather lack thereof, is a legacy of colonial rule, when getting goods out of the country took precedent over establishing a strong and lasting internal infrastructure. Neighbouring South Africa, twice the size of Mozambique, has almost 30 times more surfaced roads.

But at least the road is now passable. Just two weeks before I travel along it, this route was entirely submerged by floods, cutting Búzi and its residents off from the rest of the world. The town was among the worst-affected areas in the region. Search and rescue teams airlifted survivors from rooftops and helicopters dropped emergency food aid packages to those still trapped below. Now the water has receded, but the damage is still evident everywhere. "The things people had spent their whole life building were destroyed

⊙ Maria Bernadete, administrator of Búzi

❝

The things people had spent their whole life building were destroyed in a moment

❞

in a moment," Maria Bernadete, Búzi's softly spoken administrator, tells me.

Miguel Rabecam, the director of economic affairs at the local administration, apologises that we can't sit in his office but the roof and part of the walls have collapsed, and dust and debris have buried the desk at which he used to sit. Instead, we take a seat outside on the steps. The cyclone hit at "the worst possible moment", Rabecam tells me. He's spent the morning out in the fields assessing the damage to farmers' crops and equipment. In rural areas and small towns like Búzi, most people grow much of their own food. Mozambique's patchy road network means moving goods, particularly fresh food products, around the country is time-consuming and expensive, making subsistence farming the only financially viable option for many.

There are, broadly speaking, two harvests per year. The first, which provides staple foods like rice and cassava, was about to be collected when Cyclone Idai hit. Rabecam estimates that around three quarters of the crop in the district, much of the farmers' equipment and nearly all their livestock were lost in the flooding.

For now, food aid provided by international organisations is plugging the gap, but it's not clear how long funding will permit that to continue. Rabecam estimates that food shortages will peak between July and October 2019 and last up to a year. "If it stops, we're in big trouble. We could be looking at a famine," he says. A long queue snakes around the building for sacks of seeds. It's an attempt to replant what was lost, but Rabecam is not optimistic: "It's only going to make up for a fraction of what was destroyed. Homes can be rebuilt, but harvests can't be recovered so easily."

A perfect storm

My journey ends in Pemba city, the regional capital of Cabo Delgado, the northernmost province of Mozambique. On 25th April, Cyclone Kenneth made landfall here with wind speeds of 140 miles per hour, flattening whole neighbourhoods in its path.

In a camp for displaced people, in the Frelimo (Mozambique Liberation Front) ruling party's headquarters in Pemba, Safilna Anthony cries softly as she sits in a circle on the concrete floor with women

Harriet Salem

Harriet Salem

◐ People displaced by Cyclone Kenneth take refuge at the local headquarters of Mozambique's ruling party, the Mozambique Liberation Front, in the northern city of Pemba, 2nd May 2019

from her neighbourhood. She and her nine children were displaced from the Maluku neighbourhood in Pemba. Torrential rain caused a landslide, burying several houses in her street and partially damaging hers. "I don't want to return there. You can feel the land moving; it's not safe," she tells me as her friends nod in agreement. "We are just sitting and waiting to hear something from the government, but as yet they have not offered any solutions to our situation," another woman from the group chimes in.

They are likely to have a long wait for help from the government or aid organisations. In Cabo Delgado, home to Mozambique's lucrative gas fields, both aid relief and rebuilding efforts are being hampered by violence, thanks to an armed insurgency with an extremist Islamist ideology that is fighting a shadowy war against the state.

Starting in October 2017 the group, which has never made a public statement about its demands, began to carry out dozens of brutal attacks on villages, police stations and military outposts in the province using firebombs, guns and machetes. At least 200 people have been killed, some by beheading or dismemberment, and hundreds more are thought to have fled the rural areas of the region, where most of the attacks have taken place.

The insurgents have associations with organised criminal networks that run trafficking networks for rubies, ivory, heroin and people through Mozambique's porous border with neighbouring Tanzania. Theories abound as to what sparked the outburst of violence, but most link it in some way to the exacerbation of existing tensions by the discovery of the gas fields in the desperately poor Muslim-majority north. In particular, the increase in the state security apparatus to protect the gas fields is thought to have disrupted the thriving local black markets, which are the region's main source of income and opportunity. Heavy-handed crackdowns by the army have escalated the situation further.

With an election scheduled for 2019 the Mozambican government has been keen to keep the violence under wraps. One of activist Eric Charas's colleagues, community radio journalist Amade Abubucar, has been stuck in pre-trial detention since January after interviewing people fleeing attacks by the insurgents. Other journalists trying to cover the attacks have repeatedly been detained and had their equipment confiscated by the authorities.

As a result, few international organisations were willing to speak on the record about the impact of the violence on aid distribution in the region – all those I contacted cited fears that the government would throw them out the country if they did so. Several, however, confirmed on the condition of anonymity that the threat of attacks had hampered local access to aid and slowed down response times due to the additional risk assessments and security needed for their operations.

The fact that so little is known about the rebel group has only added to the challenge it poses. At a smart hotel on Pemba's beachfront, international aid workers meet for a nightly powwow to discuss their movements for the next day. Security concerns are top of the agenda. "You can't anticipate where a potential attack could happen, so in terms of the ground situation, we need to operate as if there are groups of armed men in the area that may kill people, be tighter with our procedures and be ready to run away at a moment's notice," a security consultant working with a major international organisation confides. "It's not the Taliban or anything like that – there's no social media, we don't know what their objective is, we don't know if we're a target or not."

Another fear is that militants may carry out reprisal attacks on villages receiving assistance, which are softer

targets. "No self-respecting jihadist group would allow international organisations to operate in their area, so obviously it's an ongoing concern that a convoy could be attacked," the security consultant tells me. "We need to keep in mind that aid adds another dynamic; it's another resource to fight over. We could also see villages attacked after we leave, which would obviously limit which areas we can operate in."

One of the few people who is willing to speak publicly to me about the appearance of the insurgency in the north is Edson Cortez, CEO of the Centre for Public Integrity, a Maputo-based anti-corruption NGO. We meet in his offices in an affluent neighbourhood of Mozambique's capital. Home to diplomats, embassies and several of the politicians that Cortez is working to expose, it's a world away from Pemba.

"In these rural regions you didn't really have the state there, then when you had these huge discoveries of gas and other natural resources in Cabo Delgado, the state had to put itself there. And the people there, involved in these scams, these criminal networks, they felt that and wanted to reassert themselves and say, 'I am here, this is mine,'" he tells me. "They are feeling robbed in these poor regions by those in power in Maputo."

"This is the problem of Mozambique," continues Cortez. "We are being run by a group of thieves and gangsters. It's hard to tell who's who. If we can't change this, if we continue down this path, then we are done for."

For his colleague Charas, the myriad issues facing Mozambique in the aftermath of Idai and Kenneth all have the same roots.

"Corruption and short-termism," he says, definitively. "That's what links all these things: the environment, cyclone damage, armed groups, poverty, infrastructure, or whatever problem it is today. It's our politics that's at the root of it all. Most of the leaders here don't care about tomorrow, just about lining their pockets – and these are the results." ⬡

⦿ Edson Cortez, CEO of the Centre for Public Integrity, a Maputo-based anti-corruption NGO

> **❝**
> We are being run by a group of thieves and gangsters. It's hard to tell who's who. If we continue down this path we are done for
> **❞**

NOTES

On the blog: To see some of the footage of the impact of the cyclones on Mozambique, visit our blog at slow-journalism.com/blog

Harriet Salem

The movie matrix

March's film releases in order of critical reception and box office success

● WORDS AND RESEARCH: **MARCUS WEBB**

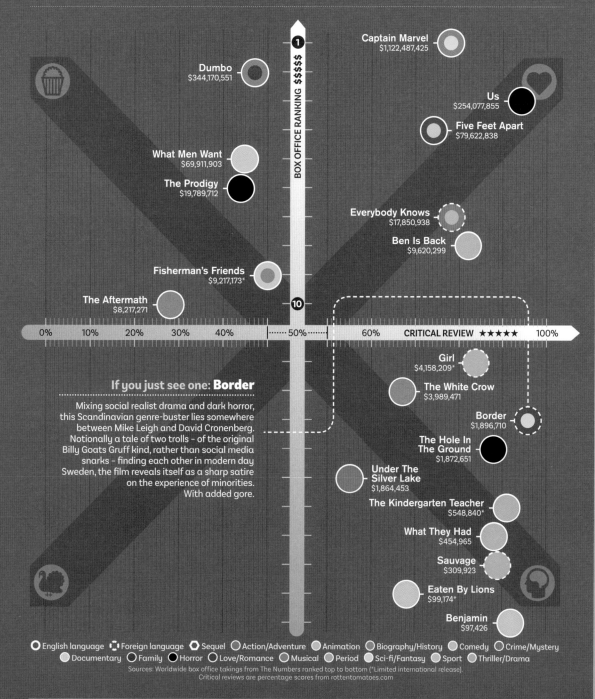

1

BOX OFFICE RANKING **$$$$$**

Captain Marvel
$1,122,487,425

Dumbo
$344,170,551

Us
$254,077,855

Five Feet Apart
$79,622,838

What Men Want
$69,911,903

The Prodigy
$19,789,712

Everybody Knows
$17,850,938

Ben Is Back
$9,620,299

Fisherman's Friends
$9,217,173*

10

The Aftermath
$8,217,271

0%   10%   20%   30%   40% ·······50%·······   60%   **CRITICAL REVIEW ★★★★★**   100%

If you just see one: **Border**

Mixing social realist drama and dark horror, this Scandinavian genre-buster lies somewhere between Mike Leigh and David Cronenberg. Notionally a tale of two trolls - of the original Billy Goats Gruff kind, rather than social media snarks - finding each other in modern day Sweden, the film reveals itself as a sharp satire on the experience of minorities. With added gore.

Girl
$4,158,209*

The White Crow
$3,989,471

Border
$1,896,710

The Hole In The Ground
$1,872,651

Under The Silver Lake
$1,864,453

The Kindergarten Teacher
$548,840*

What They Had
$454,965

Sauvage
$309,923

Eaten By Lions
$99,174*

Benjamin
$97,426

○ English language ⬚ Foreign language ◎ Sequel ○ Action/Adventure ● Animation ○ Biography/History ○ Comedy ○ Crime/Mystery
● Documentary ○ Family ● Horror ○ Love/Romance ○ Musical ● Period ● Sci-fi/Fantasy ● Sport ○ Thriller/Drama

Sources: Worldwide box office takings from The Numbers ranked top to bottom (*Limited international release).
Critical reviews are percentage scores from rottentomatoes.com

Cheat sheet

No time to read the entire issue, but want to appear as though you have?
Just scan our nine favourite facts from DG#34

You can buy an entire abandoned village in Spain with its own cinema for £214,000.
'The great baby bust', P012

The Swedish crown jewels, stolen in July 2018, were discovered seven months later in a bin with the word "bomb" written on the side.
'The art of the steal', P024

Since 1994, Warwick Davis has appeared in more of the highest grossing films of each year than any other actor.
'The Oscars vs the people', P030

The only practising foreign defence lawyer in Afghanistan once waited out a prison riot watching *Sesame Street* in a guard's hut.
'A law unto herself', P048

Before his arrest drug lord Joaquín 'El Chapo' Guzmán had his own private zoo on his estate, which he would drive people through on his own train.
'Moment that mattered' P054

An actor with no previous political experience became president of Ukraine having previously starred in a TV role as a man with no political experience who became president of Ukraine.
'The age of the ultras', P074

A single US airline is cancelling around 130 flights a day since the grounding of Boeing 737 MAX airplanes in March due to safety concerns.
'Moment that mattered', P090

Over half of the new cars sold in Norway in March 2019 were electric.
'Battery farming', P096

15th March 2019 **IDAI**
25th April 2019 **KENNETH**

Only nine storms of a tropical cyclone intensity have ever been recorded making landfall in Mozambique since records began. Two of them occurred in the first four months of 2019.
'Through hell and high water', P108